The

Mindfulness

Approach

Copyright © 2014 Dean Nelson

All rights reserved. No part of this book may be reproduced by any mechanical, photographic or electronic process, or in the form of an audio recording of any kind. This book may not be stored in a retrieval system, transmitted, or otherwise copied for public or private use, other than using brief quotations embodied in articles or reviews, without prior written permission of the publisher.

The author of this book does not dispense medical advice or prescribe the use of any technique or exercise in this book as a form of treatment for physical, mental, emotional or medical problems without the advice of a physician, either directly or indirectly. The author intends only to offer general information that may assist in your quest for spiritual, emotional or physical well-being. Should you use any information in this book for yourself, which is your constitutional right, the author and the publisher assume no responsibility for your results or for your actions.

Seven Cardinal Gates
Publishing

Acknowledgements

Dedicated to my most treasured gifts from the Universe: my daughters, Jenna and Jaclyn. As young children, you gave me the most important purpose for healing myself of ulcerative colitis. You helped me understand that I needed to put aside my pain and suffering so that I might more fully enjoy my fatherhood with you. I am forever grateful for all the love and joy you have given me throughout the years. I am so very thankful for the opportunity to enjoy sharing our lives while existing in a healthier state of being.

Thank you, Jenna Nelson, for assisting with the editing process in this book. Your perspective was refreshing, professional and greatly appreciated.

Many thanks to my wife, Paula; my daughter, Jaclyn Nelson; my brother, Van Nelson; my mom, Alice Stark; her husband, Richard Stark; Tim and Sue Raible; Chris Stricker; Debra Barnhart; and Jared Drake for each of you taking time to read my manuscript and for providing very helpful input and encouragement.

Thanks to Carsten Rieger for assisting me with the cover photo.

Special thanks to Linda Scott, LPN and Richard J. Honer, MD for reviewing my manuscript. I especially appreciate Dr. Honer allowing me to explore alternative means of medicine without being critical or discouraging me. I may not have experienced my positive healing results otherwise.

Dr. Manoj Jain, I am grateful to you for taking time out of a demanding schedule to write the preface. Your kind words and professional endorsement are greatly appreciated. Your writings for *The Washington Post*, *The New York Times*, *The* (Memphis) *Commercial Appeal* and *The Times of India* are impressive and moving. Your commitment to educating people in the ways of peace and mindfulness are touching and far reaching. It is an honor to share the experience of this book with you, and it is my sincerest intention to bring mindfulness and meditation to the hearts and minds of those who will receive it. Thank you for being a part of this journey and for your very important participation in this endeavor.

To my wife of more than 37 years: Paula, I thank you and appreciate you more than you know. You intuitively provided the information for me that would ultimately move me out of the unhealthiest state of my life. You gave me hope, inspiration and the promise of your love and support. You opened the doors that led me to the practice of meditation, which has changed me in profound ways. You have been patient, understanding and wise when I have been anxious, bull-headed and dense. Thank you, thank you, thank you!

The

Mindfulness

Approach

To Eliminate or Reduce Symptoms of Stress-Related Illnesses

Dean Nelson

Seven Cardinal Gates
Publishing

Mindfulness meditation is about finding ways of engaging and relating directly to issues in one's life by consciously and systematically taking ownership of one's health. Stress, illness, pain and any other mental, emotional or physical challenges that may beset us are our own responsibility to manage.

—Dean Nelson

Contents

Introduction   10

Preface   12

Chapter One   19
Into Darkness

Chapter Two   43
IBS, Crohn's Disease and Ulcerative Colitis: Understanding the Diseases

Chapter Three   67
What is Stress, and What Causes It?

Chapter Four   91
Reducing Stress

Chapter Five   111
Meditation

Chapter Six   **137**

A Path to a Healthy Mind and Body

Chapter Seven   **149**

A Life Fulfilled

Resources   **159**

Introduction

Manoj Jain, MD/MPH is an infectious disease physician, a writer and a national leader in healthcare quality improvement.

Dr. Jain writes regularly for *The Washington Post* and *The* (Memphis) *Commercial Appeal*. His writings have also appeared in *The New York Times* and *The Times of India*. He received his engineering, doctorate and public health degrees from Boston University. He has served as a consultant to the World Bank on HIV and has been interviewed by CNN and National Public Radio.

Over the past 15 years, Dr. Jain has given over 150 talks and published numerous scientific articles, essays and books. He has conducted research on HIV epidemiology, quality improvement and the relationship between spirituality and medicine.

Presently, Dr. Jain is adjunct assistant professor at the Rollins School of Public Health at Emory University and the medical director at Tennessee's Quality Improvement Organization, QSource (www.qsource.org).

Preface

Dean Nelson, my friend and author, has had more than a fair share of challenges in his life. As a teen, he suffered a personal tragedy—witnessing his father's suicide—which culminated in trauma-related and stress-induced health problems affecting both his body and mind for an extended period of his life. However, he found solutions, and to our benefit, he shares his secret recipe to life through his writings.

His first book, *The Experiential Approach: A Fresh New Approach for Creating Immediate Personal Power*, is designed to enhance life experiences. It is about how we can make positive changes in our behavior and thought processes by examining our beliefs, intentions, choices and actions to overcome adversity. He follows the consequential path of how beliefs lead to intentions, which create choices, which manifest into actions. If only everyone knew this.

In this book, his second, titled *The Mindfulness Approach: To Eliminate or Reduce Symptoms of*

Stress-Related Illnesses, Dean discusses how he managed his chronic health issue, ulcerative colitis, through mindfulness as taught to him by my friend and colleague Dr. Jon Kabat-Zinn. Dean elaborates on how practicing mindfulness made a remarkable difference in his life, even saving him from the scalpel.

At the onset, Dean beautifully defines mindfulness: "Mindfulness meditation is about finding ways of engaging and relating directly to issues in one's life by consciously and systematically taking ownership of one's health. Stress, illness, pain and any other mental, emotional or physical challenges that may beset us are our own responsibility to manage."

And then, he takes us on his journey.

With the help of Jon Kabat-Zinn's books and programs, Dean experienced a change. "The combination of visualization, attitude shift and daily meditation was the formula that ultimately helped bring about the massive change that I was so ready for." Soon after, Dean realizes that "Mindfulness…is a way of being. We can learn to be mindful in everything we do. Being mindful also produces extraordinary results."

I, too, am impressed by the impact of mindfulness in my life. In a *Washington Post* piece, I wrote about it.

"A few summers ago during a week-long vacation, I started playing a mind game. In the mornings, I would sit outside on a comfortable deck chair, surrounded by the shrill call of cicadas, and gaze across the lawn into the trees. After getting settled, I would close my eyes and bring my body to complete stillness except for the rhythmic rise and fall of my chest with each breath."

"Then I'd embark on what I think of as a journey with my thoughts: noticing them non-judgmentally and letting them pass through my mind like white clouds moving across the blue sky. I was practicing the very popular relaxation technique known as mindfulness."

Studies have shown that mindfulness has psychological and even some physical benefits. One 2015 meta-analysis of mindfulness-based interventions, which considered findings involving more than 8,500 participants, found that such interventions produced a decrease in depressive symptoms, anxiety and stress levels, as well as enhanced quality of life and physical functioning.

A small study in the *Journal of the American Medical Association* found that veterans with post-traumatic stress disorder who participated in an eight-week mindfulness course experienced a modest but significant decrease in symptoms compared with those given group talk therapy.

In a booklet titled *The Mindfulness Model*, which I co-wrote with Dr. Mark Muesse, a philosopher and professor at Rhodes College, we discussed how we can achieve mindfulness through meditation practices. The following is a short excerpt from the booklet.

"Hundreds of meditations can be categorized in three broad categories. Focused Attention or Anchoring Meditation: when we focus on an object or activity such as our breathing or visualizing an image. Open Monitoring or Surveying Meditation: when we observe our mind without any judgment. Self-transcendence or Relinquishing Thought Meditation: when we go into a state of dwindling thoughts."

"Living in a mindful state can transform our day-to-day lives. Mindfulness can bring five transformations. First, physical and mental wellness. Scientific studies show meditation leads to longevity, lower blood pressure, a stronger immune system and less depression. Second, peace. Anger, violence and hate in our thoughts, speech and actions dissipate when one becomes more self-aware. Third, compassion. We can evolve from emotions of pity to sympathy to empathy to compassion through a mindful state. Fourth, wisdom and insight. Wisdom is the ability to see things as they are. One can do this though insight, which comes when we see reality from multiple perspectives. Fifth, spirituality and religiosity.

Connecting to a higher power or to a deeper self through the teachings of ancient religious traditions or simply through self-reflection."

"Ultimately, these transformations impact our life in a profound way as experienced by sages of the past and present. They bring us happiness, where happiness is not pleasure; rather it is contentment, fulfillment and meaning and purpose in life."

If we wish to make a change, as Dean helps us realize in his engaging book, we need to be receptive. Then life challenges us. He candidly writes, "I was not an open-minded person at the time, but I was desperate and willing to do whatever it took to turn my sickly life around."

This book will help us make the change we wish to be.

The Mindfulness Approach

Chapter One

Into Darkness

When a miserably unhealthy physical condition manifested itself in my life at an early age, I realized that my life was not going according to what I had envisioned. Fear and discouragement began to root themselves in my mind, and the abundant dreams I had cradled for a happy, healthy life began slipping away into darkness.

Stress, ulcerative colitis, irritable bowel syndrome (IBS) and Crohn's disease can have devastating life-long effects on people of any age. For me, the grim journey began shortly after I witnessed my father's horrific suicide when I was at home alone with him at the impressionable age of 15.

The stress of dealing with my father's untimely death, along with the typical trials and turbulence of my rapidly changing youthful life, took its toll on my health. I found myself deeply depressed, and I felt lost and hopelessly abandoned for many years.

At about age 19, I began to experience the first repulsive symptoms of ulcerative colitis. There was occasional blood and mucous in my stools along with a visceral cramping pain and discomfort. I tried not to worry about it as the symptoms were only occurring every few weeks, but over the course of a couple of years, they became progressively worse until I finally decided to seek professional help.

The first doctor who I visited was our family practitioner at the time. His diagnosis was ulcerative colitis, and he informed me that I was far too young to be experiencing enough stress to cause this atrocious disease to manifest. His advice was to shy away from fried foods and spicy meals. I did make a half-hearted attempt to adjust my eating habits, but it did not seem to make much of a difference.

Over the next several years, the episodes became more intense and frequent. There were times when I could eat just about anything without negative recourse and other times when it seemed that the slightest misstep would push my sensitive digestive system over the edge. It wasn't until much later that I learned, essentially, that it is not so much what we eat that causes the symptoms; it is more what is eating us!

I was plagued by guilt about my father's heart-rending suicide. Being somewhat of a free-spirited teenager, I was desperately trying to find my way in this uncertain world in ways that did not meet with my father's expectations. He disapproved of my long hair and the friends I had chosen. I was tormented with the fear of failing as I felt my father had also failed by abruptly ending his life. I struggled dreadfully with countless thoughts of suicide myself throughout those burdensome years.

On the surface, I'm sure I seemed emotionally stable to those around me for the most part, but underneath I was seething with emotional distress. Being attracted to and marrying the perfect woman for me and having two wonderful children was probably the best thing that could have happened to me at the time. Despite the multitude of new concerns that can arise during the first few years of marriage, having children can cause an enormous amount of stress for many people. My close family unit was what kept me fighting vehemently for my life.

Paula, my wife of 37 years, and my two daughters are my biggest sources of joy. Paula was instrumental in bringing about a massive change toward good health and happiness in my life. A healthy mind is a healthy body, and I am living proof of this.

By the time I was 35 or so, ulcerative colitis had consumed the better part of my life and had become my absolute worst enemy. One evil detail about colitis is that the more stress you encounter, the worse your symptoms get. The worse your symptoms get, the more stress you encounter. It was a cycle that seemed impossible to defeat at the time, so I sought out another local doctor who referred me to a colon and rectal surgeon, Dr. Richard J. Honer.

Dr. Honer is not only a great doctor; he is a great humanitarian. He has been awarded the Physician's Humanitarian Award for his more than 15 years of service to the Dominican Republic, and he devotes time each week to providing free medical services to local indigent patients here in Florida who would not otherwise be able to afford treatment.

During my first couple of years in his care, Dr. Honer prescribed various medicines, beginning with those that exhibited the fewest side effects. However, I seemed to become immune to each of the medications, and my symptoms became progressively worse, so he began to prescribe more potent medicines.

Ulcerative colitis was cyclical for me as it is for many afflicted people. I would experience a sobering outbreak that would last a week or two, and I would be thoroughly miserable during that time. Then the symptoms would subside and vanish overnight. For the next few days, I would feel cautiously great and would sometimes believe that the revolting disease had run its course and I was home free.

Then, like a sonic boom, a full-blown flare-up would disrupt my life in an instant, and I would be thrown into a miserably ravaged state of pain and discomfort. Anyone with ulcerative colitis, Crohn's Disease or Irritable Bowel Syndrome knows this uncomfortably horrid feeling. Bouncing back and forth between distressing loose stools and intolerable constipation was another discouraging facet of the disease, not to mention the extreme loss of energy.

Most of the time it felt like I had swallowed a bowling ball and it had embedded itself in the pit of my stomach where it resided for the duration of the flare up. The constant urge to eliminate was incredibly bothersome and it engendered incremental stress that only led to exacerbated symptoms.

There were times I would make eight or ten embarrassing trips to the restroom during the course of one hour. It felt as though a bowel movement was forthcoming but only gas, blood and mucus would be excreted. This repulsive condition interfered with my job more than I care to remember. I was continually accused of retreating to my "second office" many times during each day when I was experiencing these flare ups.

The pain and cramping was almost easier to deal with than the frustration of not being able to complete tasks without constant interruptions at work. Of course, this only added to the stress levels. I could not wait to get home so I could frequent the restroom without the embarrassment of other's wondering why I was spending so much time in there at work. It was a humiliating experience and it created so much more stress for me and made enduring the symptoms that much more difficult.

I had to carefully plan for my whereabouts each day timing trips to the store so I would have just enough time to either find a restroom or make it back to work or home before the next urge established itself. Yes, there were times when I could not make it back in time or find an available restroom and it caused me to pass gas along with blood and mucus in my underwear. I would have to make occasional emergency trips home to make a change. I then began to bring extra underwear with me just in case.

There were so many times I had to literally run to the restroom in fear of soiling my pants. It was a miserably fearful time to work or play. There were many events I would miss due to not being sure if there were restrooms on site that were clean and available for use. Often I would make numerous trips to the restroom and would be missed for extended periods of time. I would want to make sure I had eliminated as much blood and mucus as I could before returning to the people I was with. Of course, I would be interrogated as to why I was gone for so long and I did not want to divulge my ugly secret.

Company and family dinners were scary times for me. I would always scope out the nearest restrooms and check to see if there were enough stalls available just in case there were others using it at the time. I would seek out other restrooms that may be available in the vicinity. Many times I would have to run to another store or restaurant if the restroom was occupied at the place where I was at the time.

Fastidious planning would be involved with every trip anywhere. I would always make sure there were fast food restaurants or grocery stores along the way. Apologizing to family and friends for stopping along the way even on short trips to nearby towns became the norm. It discouraged me from wanting to go anywhere during flare ups. I made more excuses for not going places that I really wanted to go to due to this monstrous disease.

Flare ups would last anywhere from two or three days to a week or more. Usually, after five or six days the symptoms would subside and I would experience normal life for about the same periods of time as the flare ups. I cannot express the utter joy and relief when normalcy made its way back into my life. I was always so hopeful each time a flare up would end that the disease had finally regressed and then I would be able to enjoy life without the constant fear of its return a few days later. It was a roller coaster ride of mental anguish and physical pain and discomfort.

One of the most difficult elements was not knowing when a flare up would occur. It would happen at a moment's notice and foil well made plans. I would rather have not been around anyone when I was feeling ill and this made life so difficult. I never wanted anyone to know about this embarrassing disorder. Why would I want someone to know how disgusting these symptoms were? How would I describe it if they were to ask? It altered the entire course of my life for quite some time.

The only reason I am sharing the explicit details now is so you will understand how I felt and so you may relate to these symptoms or the symptoms you may be experiencing with your health concern. I am guessing you are reading this book because you are now suffering or have suffered in the past with a traumatic experience, a mental or physical disease or a disorder of some sort.

Even if you are not currently experiencing Ulcerative Colitis, Crohn's disease or IBS, you may benefit tremendously from the information in this book. I am convinced that the path I undertook to reverse the symptoms of ulcerative colitis can also reverse the symptoms of many other stress-induced diseases. In fact, there is a great deal of information available to support this. I will explore this information later in the book.

The Tipping Point

When Dr. Honer mentioned to me that surgery is required in many cases for patients who do not respond favorably to the medications, I became extremely fearful. I had been on various medications for extended periods of time, and my condition was becoming worse as time passed. My mind was filled with thoughts of how I would cope with these life-altering circumstances.

For me, fear was a big motivator at the time. I was young and active with a wife and two daughters who I adored, and I had no intention of letting this disease devour my colon. There was significant damage to my colon already, but Dr. Honer felt it could be saved if it did not get worse. I had to find a way to reverse this disease and rid myself of these nightmarish conditions.

Fortunately for me, my wife was very open-minded and decided that I should seek alternative methods of medicine. Her superior intuition always guides her to make choices that benefit others. While in a bookstore one day, she intuitively discovered a book by Jon Kabat-Zinn, Ph.D. entitled *Full Catastrophe Living: Using the Wisdom of the Body and Mind to Face Stress, Pain and Illness.*

Jon Kabat-Zinn, Ph.D. is Emeritus Professor of Medicine at the University of Massachusetts Medical School and founding director of the school's Stress Reduction Clinic and the Center for Mindfulness in Medicine, Health Care and Society. He pioneered the concept of mind-body medicine back in the 70s and has been an incredibly positive influence on mainstream medicine ever since.

Full Catastrophe Living was instrumental in helping me bring about the changes that I needed to make. It helped me to relax into life and let go of some of my haunting past so that I could allow my body to do what it should do naturally: heal itself!

The book basically mirrors the eight-week program that Dr. Kabat-Zinn was running at the time at the Stress Reduction Clinic at the University of Massachusetts Medical Center. According to the University of Massachusetts website, more than 20,000 people from all walks of life have completed the program, and the findings of three decades of published research indicate that the majority of people who complete the course report the following:

- Lasting decreases in physical and psychological symptoms
- An increased ability to relax
- Reductions in pain levels and an enhanced ability to cope with pain that may not go away
- Greater energy and enthusiasm for life
- Improved self-esteem
- An ability to cope more effectively with both short- and long-term stress

Mindfulness meditation is about finding ways of engaging and relating directly to issues in one's life by consciously and systematically taking ownership of one's health. Stress, illness, pain and any other mental, emotional or physical challenges that may beset us are our own responsibility to manage.

I ordered the Mindfulness Meditation program by Dr. Kabat-Zinn, which was just a couple of cassette tapes at the time, and this proved to be very beneficial. I enjoy guided meditations and, to this day, continue to use the Body Scan technique. I still find it easy to fall into step with the program and allow the message to take me along the guided journey. The Body Scan was a favorite of mine. I participated with it many times and found the effects to be strangely realistic and wonderful.

This book clearly demonstrates how mindfulness meditation not only creates a strategy for a balanced mind and a healthy body but that it is easy to follow the book's instructions for learning the meditation process. There are a variety of meditation practices discussed in his book, including yoga, sitting and walking meditations and the Body Scan.

Dr. Kabat-Zinn makes scientific discussions of the relationship between stress and illness—and the incredible power of the mind to bring about healing and recovery—in simple, easy-to-understand terms.

In short, this book has changed my life. It offered me an alternative to the harsh medicines and possible future surgery. It relieved me of the miserable symptoms I described earlier as well as the extremely stressful conditions the disease placed on my family, business and social lives. It offered me a way out of the downward spiral of physical, emotional and mental deterioration that I was experiencing.

The Way Out

What helped me trust the meditation process even more was the fact that Dr. Kabat-Zinn was featured in Bill Moyers' PBS Special, "Healing and the Mind." It was a fantastic program that made me understand more fully the mind-body connection and how I could use that information to create an effective mind-body healing experience.

Dr. Honer was thoughtful and open-minded enough to look at a video copy of the program I had received from PBS for a donation to their programming efforts. I am not really sure how sold he was on the information at the time, but he encouraged me to move forward and use whatever techniques and alternative means I encountered that could possibly make a difference.

The Stress Reduction Clinic's program involved about an hour's time each day. This was a tall commitment for me since I was working 60–70 hours per week at my job in the automobile industry. However, the fear within me quickly helped me decide to sacrifice time away from the TV and to get up earlier than usual to find the time to meditate.

Jon Kabat-Zinn mentions in the beginning of the book that it does not matter whether you believe the meditative process will work or not. He said that if one just disciplines one's self and follows the program through to completion, the results will speak for themselves.

I was not an open-minded person at the time, but I was desperate and willing to do whatever it took to turn my sickly life around. However, I became extremely open-minded during the process when I began to see results.

The meditation process does not discriminate on the basis of race, gender, social status, religious affiliation or health conditions. It works, really, without any effort at all. It is about non-doing rather than attempting to accomplish a specific goal. It is in the letting go and the allowing that the body responds with a relaxing, stress-reducing healing experience.

The practice could probably work for anyone but will likely only work for those who can be consistent and follow the principles of the techniques without expectations. It is in the stilling of the mind and the body that relaxation and stress reduction combine to allow the healing processes to operate as they were intended.

I was desperate and frustrated with my life-altering health conditions and willing to do whatever it took to bring my life back to a normal, functional way of being. Overall, I consumed a healthy diet, clinging to health foods, vitamins and supplements for many years. It was not the diet that had let me down; it was my emotional state that left me in the pangs of ill health.

By this time, I felt as though I had paid the price for my lack of attention to my emotional health. After all the years of eating well and paying close attention to healthy foods and supplements that were colitis-friendly, I finally realized that none of that regimen mattered much at all. It was my mental and emotional states that were harboring issues from the past that needed to be observed and released.

"What the mind harbors, the body manifests," is a favorite quote of mine from the audio series *The Psychology of Winning* by Denis Waitley, a best-selling author and lecturer. This audio program was also instrumental in developing within me an understanding of how the mind-body connection operates and in what ways I could alter my thinking and behavior patterns to achieve a more balanced, relaxed approach to life.

The series assisted me in establishing an attitude of positive self-expectancy which became a standard in my everyday living. Expecting positive outcomes feels far better than the alternative. I began to use visualization techniques to enhance my daily meditation practice and help bring this positive influence into my moment-to-moment awareness.

I asked Dr. Honer for some illustrations of the intestinal tract and colon area, and he graciously provided these. The idea of the visualization was to use a green highlighter to mark the area of difficulty in my colon and visualize the green highlight as healing energy moving through the area. Once I studied the pictures a number of times, I was able to recreate the image in my mind throughout each day whenever I would get a chance. Of course, I had many opportunities each day as I headed for the restroom.

The combination of visualization, attitude shift and daily meditation was the formula that ultimately helped bring about the massive change that I was so ready for.

Guided meditations are meditations performed while listening to the voice of the instructor, who takes one through the meditative experience utilizing visualization techniques. To this day, I still enjoy guided meditations.

With the advent of YouTube and other video-sharing platforms on the internet, there are far more guided meditations available today than there were 30 years ago. The videos can be visually stunning and include technologies such as brain-wave synchronization, entrainment and binaural beats.

Affirmations were also a part of my regular routine; however, I did not find them to be an effective means of change. The problem with affirmations, when spoken or read, can be that the mind automatically knows they may be untrue.

For example, if I used the affirmation, "My body is healthy and free of colitis symptoms," the response from my brain would likely be, "Liar! That is untrue!" No matter how many times I would repeat such a phrase, it still resonated as an untruth.

Affirmations and visualizations are very different in nature. There are times when you can trick the mind as it does not always know the difference between what is vividly imagined and what is actual reality. Deep, vivid visualizations can deceive the brain so you can create a desirable feeling and picture, in your mind, the state of being healthy and disease free. But as soon as you return to normal waking consciousness, the realty of your state of health can become all too real once again.

I'm sure affirmations can be beneficial if used on a regular basis for the purposes of positive thinking. However, those positive affirmations may still be interpreted as untrue and, at some level, a person will resist the statements. I have since then learned that affirmations can be more effective when used as beliefs that are created in a slightly different way.

For instance, if I altered the above affirmation to say, "My body is <u>on its way to becoming</u> healthy and free of colitis symptoms," this would be more believable and readily accepted by my mind as a possibility. Even though I may still have relapses, the possibility that I am on my way towards healing is more palatable than the fact that I am not yet free from the disease.

I can more readily believe that healing is a process and understand that it may take some time for it to manifest. The Universe has its own timing. When I am doing my part to bring this to fruition, using the very best tools of meditation and visualization while trusting that it will come about in time, I am in a superior position to allow the healing to take place.

People have contrasting ideas about The Law of Attraction, its origins, and how it works. Basically, it appears to relate to ancient concepts of "like attracts like." The modern, more popular version of the Law of Attraction states that you *Ask* the Universe (Creator, God, Source, Higher Self, the God of your heart—however you personally reference this) for what you want, *Believe* with unwavering faith that is it yours and *Receive* it with joy and gratitude.

The Universe may grant one's request instantly, but it also may take days, weeks, months or years depending on the individual's level of belief and state of being.

If one is not in a mindset of absolute allowing, while also feeling that he or she is deserving of the request and is personally responsible for the results, then that person may never receive it at all. Taking complete responsibility for our own physical, mental, emotional and spiritual health and well-being is paramount to any positive transformation.

The next chapter is dedicated to those who suffer from IBS, ulcerative colitis or Crohn's Disease. If you have no issues with any of these conditions, you may skip chapter two and continue with chapter three.

However, many people suffer from IBS and do not recognize its symptoms. Gastroesophageal reflux disease (GERD), more commonly referred to as acid reflux, is associated with IBS.

Chapter Two

IBS, Crohn's Disease and Ulcerative Colitis:
Understanding the Diseases

According to the International Foundation for Functional Gastrointestinal Disorders (IFFGD), IBS is the most common gastrointestinal (GI) disorder worldwide. Prevalence rates around the world range from nine to twenty-three percent, with the U.S. coming in at around ten to fifteen percent.

Approximately thirty-five to forty percent of those reporting IBS symptoms are male and around sixty to sixty-five percent are female. IFFGD considers IBS a major women's health issue.

The Crohn's and Colitis Foundation of America reports that 1.4 million Americans have Crohn's disease or ulcerative colitis. Of those, about 700,000 have Crohn's disease. Sadly, most cases are diagnosed before the age of 30. The ratio is about even between males and females.

IBS

Let's first discuss the usually less problematic of the inflammatory bowel diseases, referred to as IBS. Some studies estimate that as much as 20 percent of the adult population is affected by IBS, but most studies cite a range of 10 to 15 percent.

Technically, IBS is classified as a functional GI disorder and is not considered a disease, although its symptoms are similar to that of ulcerative colitis and Crohn's disease in that sufferers exhibit abdominal pain or discomfort, excess gas or bloating, cramping, diarrhea, constipation or any combination thereof.

However, IBS is quite different from ulcerative colitis and Crohn's disease. Though its symptoms are similar, it is usually a far less serious condition. IBS is a functional disorder that affects the motility (muscle contractions) of the colon and is not generally characterized by intestinal inflammation. Many have referred to it as spastic colon, colitis, nervous colitis, mucous colitis and nervous colon, although it bears no direct relationship to either ulcerative colitis or Crohn's disease.

Uniformity was achieved when the condition was renamed "IBS" to reflect the current understanding that the disorder seems to result from a combination of physical and mental health problems. However, the actual causes remain a mystery and are not well understood. The National Institute of Diabetes and Digestive and Kidney Diseases lists some possible causes of IBS:

- **Brain-gut signal problems.** Signals between the brain and nerves of the small and large intestines, also called the gut, control how the intestines work. Problems with brain-gut signals may cause IBS symptoms, such as changes in bowel habits and pain or discomfort.

- **GI motor problems.** Normal motility, or movement, may not be present in the colon of a person who has IBS. Slow motility can lead to constipation and fast motility can lead to diarrhea. Spasms, or sudden strong muscle contractions that come and go, can cause abdominal pain. Some people with IBS also experience hyperactivity, which is an excessive increase in contractions of the bowel in response to stress or eating.

- **Hypersensitivity.** People with IBS have a lower pain threshold to the stretching of the bowel caused by gas or stool compared with people who do not have IBS. The brain may process pain signals from the bowel differently in people with IBS.

- **Mental health problems.** Mental health problems, such as panic disorder, anxiety, depression and post-traumatic stress disorder are common in people with IBS. The link between these disorders and development of IBS is unclear. GI disorders, including IBS, are often found in people who have reported past physical or sexual abuse. Researchers believe that people who have been abused tend to express psychological stress through physical symptoms.

- **Bacterial gastroenteritis.** Some people who have bacterial gastroenteritis—an infection or irritation of the stomach and intestines caused by bacteria—develop IBS. Researchers do not know why gastroenteritis leads to IBS in some people and not others, though psychological problems and abnormalities of the lining of the GI tract may be factors.

- **Small intestinal bacterial overgrowth (SIBO).** Normally, few bacteria live in the small intestine. SIBO is an increase in the number of bacteria or a change in the type of bacteria in the small intestine. These bacteria can produce excess gas and may also cause diarrhea and weight loss. Some researchers believe that SIBO may lead to IBS, and some studies have shown antibiotics to be effective in treating IBS. However, the studies' findings were weak, and more research is needed to verify a link between SIBO and IBS.

- **Body chemicals.** People with IBS have altered levels of neurotransmitters, which are chemicals in the body that transmit nerve signals and GI hormones, though the role these chemicals play in developing IBS is unclear. Younger women with IBS often have more symptoms during their menstrual periods. Post-menopausal women have fewer symptoms compared with women who are still menstruating. These findings suggest that reproductive hormones can worsen IBS problems.

- **Genetics.** Whether IBS has a genetic cause, meaning that it runs in families, is unclear. Studies have shown that IBS is more common in people with family members who have a history of GI problems. However, the cause could be environmental or the result of heightened awareness of GI symptoms.

- **Food sensitivity.** Many people with IBS report that certain foods and beverages can cause symptoms, such as foods rich in carbohydrates, spicy or fatty foods, coffee and alcohol. However, people with food sensitivity typically do not have clinical signs of a food allergy. Researchers have proposed that symptoms may result from poor absorption of sugars or bile acids, which help break down fats and get rid of waste in the body.

Some people may experience only mild symptoms of IBS while others will have severe symptoms and may find the condition disabling. Medical treatment will not necessarily alleviate symptoms. It is always best to discuss your symptoms with your doctor because the symptoms of IBS can also be indicators of serious diseases such as ulcerative colitis, Crohn's disease or cancer. It is also possible that you may have an infection.

See your doctor if you are experiencing a persistent change in bowel habits or have any signs or symptoms of IBS. Your doctor will want to rule out any serious diseases or infections and may be able to prescribe medications or a change in diet to relieve your symptoms.

IBS is a chronic condition for most people, with symptoms that become worse at times and then quickly improve or disappear altogether.

There is no known cure, and the cause is elusive. The intestine's walls are layered with muscles that contract and relax in a synergistic rhythm while moving food from your stomach all the way through your intestinal tract to your rectum.

A person with IBS may experience longer and stronger contractions, causing food to be forced along through their intestines far too quickly. This results in gas, bloating and diarrhea.

Conversely, the contractions may occur too slowly, causing stools to become hard and dry and thus resulting in pain and discomfort. The intestinal walls become bloated and stretched with the formation of excess gas.

The Mayo Clinic lists IBS triggers, which affect some people and not others. Some may react strongly to stimuli that do not bother others. According to the Mayo Clinic, these triggers can range from gas pressure in the intestinal tract to specific foods, medications or emotional matters.

Here are the possible triggers listed:

- **Foods.** Many people find that their signs and symptoms worsen when they eat certain foods. For instance, chocolate, milk and alcohol might cause constipation or diarrhea. Carbonated beverages and some fruits and vegetables may lead to bloating and discomfort in some people with IBS. The role of food allergy or intolerance in IBS has yet to be clearly understood.

  If you experience cramping and bloating mainly after eating dairy products, food with caffeine, or sugar-free gum or candies, the problem may not be IBS. Instead, your body may not be able to tolerate the sugar (lactose) in dairy products, caffeine or the artificial sweetener sorbitol.

- **Stress.** If you're like most people with IBS, you probably find that your signs and symptoms are worse or more frequent during stressful events, such as a change in your daily routine. But while stress may aggravate symptoms, it doesn't cause them.

- **Hormones.** Because women are more likely to have IBS, researchers believe that hormonal changes play a role in this condition. Many women find that signs and symptoms are worse during or around their menstrual periods.

Another serious condition associated with IBS is GERD, more commonly known as acid reflux. This condition reveals itself when acidic stomach contents find their way back up through the esophagus toward the throat. This condition is related to the muscle between the esophagus and the stomach being weak or relaxing when it should not.

IBS is a functional GI disorder. These symptoms manifest themselves because of changes in how the GI tract operates. Once again, IBS is not a disease. It is a disorder made up of a number of symptoms that occur individually or in unison.

Non-GI conditions can also be found alongside IBS symptoms.

Chronic fatigue syndrome is one of these. It's a disorder that can cause extreme fatigue that may persist for long periods of time and limit one's ability to perform simple tasks and daily activities.

Temporomandibular joint (TMJ) disorders are also on the list. These concern problems with the chewing muscles and joints connecting the lower jaw to the skull.

Anxiety, depression and pelvic pain are related as well. Somatoform disorders, also included in the lineup, involve chronic pain or other symptoms with no apparent physical cause and are believed to be due to psychological problems.

Treating IBS

Foods that are low in fat—fruits, vegetables, cereals, whole grain breads and rice—may help. Gradually increasing fiber in the diet, drinking plenty of water and exercising consistently may reduce constipation and stress. One may benefit greatly by eating meals slowly in a relaxed environment.

Symptoms of IBS can be treated with a combination of medications, probiotics, altered eating habits, diet and nutritional intake, as well as mental health therapy and, of course, meditation. Consult your doctor if you suspect a wheat allergy, lactose intolerance or celiac disease, which may exhibit similar symptoms to IBS.

Eating large meals can trigger cramping with diarrhea or constipation. It may be beneficial to eat several, smaller meals throughout the day or partake in smaller portion sizes in general.

Trigger foods for many people include fried foods, foods with a high fat and/or sugar content, alcoholic beverages, carbonated or caffeinated drinks, certain dairy products and chocolate.

Other problematic foods that may cause gas and irritation are beans, cabbages, Brussels sprouts, broccoli, onions and the artificial sweeteners sorbitol and xylitol.

Limiting or eliminating some or all of these foods and beverages may reduce symptoms and provide relief from pain and discomfort. Each individual's body and psychological state is different and will respond to dietary revisions differently.

I have read many stories of people who have eliminated all of their symptoms of IBS and ulcerative colitis by means of dietary modifications alone. This did not work for me with ulcerative colitis; however, I would highly recommend a combination of changing one's diet while implementing a meditation routine of some sort to reduce stress. Of course, see your doctor first for a proper diagnosis and treatment plan.

There are many nerve endings in the colon that connect to the brain. The normal contractions used to move food through the tract are controlled by these nerves. The communication between the brain and the colon can be intensified under stress, and the colon may become overly responsive to even a slight increase in stress levels, causing spasms and abdominal discomfort.

Stress can actually create a greater mental awareness of the sensations that are experienced within the colon. When these sensations intensify, the individual experiences more stress. When the individual experiences more stress, the sensations intensify to a greater degree. The cycle continues until the stress is reduced and a more peaceful state of being is attained.

The National Digestive Diseases Information Clearinghouse, a division of the Department of Health and Human Services, offers these options for managing stress:

- Participate in stress reduction and relaxation therapies, such as meditation.
- Get counseling and support.
- Take part in regular exercise, such as walking or yoga.
- Minimize stressful life situations as much as possible.

- Get enough sleep.

If you require medical treatment, your doctor will determine your treatment plan based on your symptoms and your physical and emotional condition.

Crohn's Disease vs. Ulcerative Colitis

Crohn's disease was named after Dr. Burrill B. Crohn who, in 1932, described the disease as belonging to a group of conditions known as inflammatory bowel diseases, or IBD. Crohn's disease is a chronic inflammatory condition of the gastrointestinal tract. Dr. Crohn observed his findings with his colleagues, Dr. Leon Ginzburg and Dr. Gordon D. Oppenheimer.

Crohn's disease and ulcerative colitis are the two most common types of IBD. Their similarities involve causing abnormal responses from the body's immune system.

Typically, white blood cells protect the body from infection, but with IBD, the immune system may mistake materials such as food and beneficial bacteria in the intestines for foreign invading substances.

The immune system may then launch an attack on the cells of the intestines by deploying white blood cells into the intestinal lining, where chronic inflammation and the symptoms of IBDs are experienced.

Even though the symptoms may be similar, they affect different areas of the GI tract.

Crohn's most commonly affects the ilium, the small bowel and the beginning of the colon. However, it may affect any portion of the GI from the mouth to the anus whereas ulcerative colitis is more limited to the large intestine (colon).

Ulcerative colitis only involves the inner lining of the colon as opposed to Crohn's, which commonly affects the entire thickness of the bowel wall and may bounce from one area to another, distressing various sections of the intestine.

The Centers for Disease Control and Prevention (CDC), cites symptoms related to Crohn's disease:

- Persistent diarrhea
- Rectal bleeding
- Urgent need to move bowels
- Abdominal cramps and pain
- Sensation of incomplete evacuation
- Constipation (can lead to bowel obstruction)

General symptoms that may also be associated with other IBDs are as follows:

- Fever
- Loss of appetite
- Weight loss
- Fatigue
- Night sweats
- Loss of normal menstrual cycle

These symptoms are very similar to those of ulcerative colitis; some of them are similar to symptoms of IBS. Also similar to ulcerative colitis is the fact that Crohn's patients will more than likely experience periods of flare-ups followed by remissions where the patient experiences normalcy.

Both conditions can cause a patient to experience tears, referred to as fissures, in the lining of the anus which can cause bleeding along with pain and discomfort.

Fistulas—which are tunnels within the body's tissue, in this case often occurring between loops in the intestines—may also develop, causing further complications. Fistulas can form between the intestine, bladder, vagina or skin. These conditions are serious and require medical attention and often surgery.

With Crohn's, a common complication is a blockage within the intestine resulting from swelling and residual scar tissue. This can cause severe cramping and vomiting and must be treated immediately.

Crohn's affects people of all ages while being more prominent among women than men. Both Crohn's and ulcerative colitis are diagnosed predominately in patients between the ages of 15 and 35. The risk of acquiring a type of bowel cancer is elevated in Crohn's and ulcerative colitis patients.

Common symptoms of ulcerative colitis are these:

- Abdominal pain and discomfort
- Fatigue
- Fever
- Nausea
- Weight loss
- Loss of appetite
- Blood and/or mucous in the stool
- Loss of body fluids and nutrients
- Diarrhea
- Growth failure in children

Other symptoms that may be related to ulcerative colitis include eye irritation, kidney stones, joint pain, liver disease and osteoporosis.

Treating Crohn's and Ulcerative Colitis

Dietary changes may be recommended depending on the patient's symptoms, medications and possible reactions to certain foods or food groups.

Most ulcerative colitis and Crohn's patients should avoid fried or greasy foods that are high in fat, carbonated beverages and some dairy products. They should also limit alcohol consumption, eat smaller meals, drink plenty of fluids and consider taking multivitamins.

Treatment may also include the use of medication and/or procedures to repair or remove affected portions of the GI tract.

Medication for inflammation of the colon due to these diseases can suppress the symptoms and allow the tissues to heal. Medication can control and suppress symptoms and cause ulcerative colitis or Crohn's to go into remission and reduce the frequency of flare-ups over time.

There are a number of medications available today that may be quite effective for treating these diseases. However, when medications fail to produce positive results, surgery may be required.

Unfortunately, the statistics are not favorable. According to the Crohn's and Colitis Foundation of America, nearly 70 percent of Crohn's patients will eventually require surgery which, ultimately, may not eliminate all symptoms.

Approximately 30 percent of patients who underwent surgery experienced a recurrence of their symptoms within three years. Sixty percent will have symptoms recur within 10 years. These disturbing statistics shed light on the fact that there is no known cure for Crohn's disease.

About 25 to 30 percent of ulcerative colitis patients will require surgery at some point. A cure for ulcerative colitis would be to remove the colon and/or rectum and create an ileostomy—an external opening on the abdomen. An ostomy pouching system will be required. The colostomy bag is then attached to the skin and is used to collect solid waste.

However, surgical techniques have become so advanced that many patients are now able to choose a procedure that removes the colon but avoids the ileostomy.

The surgeon creates an internal pouch from the small bowel and attaches it to the anal sphincter muscle. This eliminates the need for the patient to wear the ostomy pouch and preserves the integrity of the bowel.

Other Options

IBS, Crohn's disease or ulcerative colitis may have physical, mental or emotional origins, and the option to pursue alternative means of pain relief, remission or healing remains available to all.

If one is open and willing to learn techniques and processes that have been proven to reduce stress and calm the mind and body while engendering states of being that are more conducive to healthy living, they may then experience physical, mental and/or emotional healing.

Learning to manage stress alone may precipitate the greatest, most effective means of easing symptoms, relieving pain and inducing remission or, at the very least, promoting avenues for learning to live with pain and discomfort.

Chapter Three

What is Stress, and What Causes It?

Stress is merely a reaction to any number of stimuli that interrupt our physical or mental equilibrium. It is a physical, mental or emotional tension resulting from adverse or undesirable circumstances. It can be anything that presents a threat or challenge to our well-being.

Common stressors can be personal conflicts, health issues, financial problems, unexpected changes in plans, auto accidents, job changes, marital or relationship differences, emergency situations, making mistakes and guilt over concealing information, troubling ourselves with what others may think of us and countless other worries, including the most trivial of issues.

According to Health Advocate, Inc., the nation's leading healthcare advocacy and assistance company, regarding a survey conducted in 2007, nearly three-quarters of American workers reported experiencing physical symptoms of stress due to work.

They also cited statistics from the American Psychological Association (APA) showing that a disturbing two-thirds of Americans state that work is the main source of stress in their lives. That figure was up nearly 15 percent from those who ranked work as the primary just a year prior. Approximately 30 percent of workers surveyed reported "extreme" stress levels.

Health Advocate states that, whatever the root causes, stressed workers tend to be fatigued, prone to mistakes and injuries and are more likely to be absent.

The most significant findings inform us of healthcare costs reaching more than double that of other employees. The costs of stress-related illnesses incurred by American businesses is estimated between $200 to $300 *billion* a year in lost productivity.

It is easy to see that controlling our levels of stress can have positive effects on our financial situations. Less absenteeism in our jobs could equate to more income, less stress could provide more focus, creativity and attention to details for increased productivity, and less medical bills would translate into more disposable income.

Basically, there are three types of stress: Acute, Episodic Acute and Chronic. Let's explore these for a moment.

Acute Stress

Acute Stress is the most common, resulting from demands and pressures placed on oneself involving the recent past along with anticipated demands and pressures of the impending future. Acute Stress can be exciting and rewarding in short doses, but an overabundance may cause frustration and exhaustion.

A short dose of rewarding stress may be found in the following example. Let's say, you decide to participate in a 5K run early one summer morning. The temperature is warm but bearable. You are running with friends, and the only real competition is between yourself and your prior running times. So, the pressure (stress) is on you and motivates you to perform so that you will impress your friends and surpass your former race times. It is a good temporary motivator.

Another scenario might involve an overdose of Acute Stress. Let's say the 5K run is held late in the afternoon in summer, when it is very hot. Your boss demands that you work all day prior to the event and push yourself as hard as you can to get your work completed in time to leave early. You are not only competing with yourself but with another runner who always finishes ahead of you and gloats openly while directing verbal jabs toward your inability to beat him.

In this situation, you are already tired from your boss pushing you, all the work you performed earlier that day and the fact that it is very hot outside in the afternoon. In addition, you are racing against an adversary that will disgrace you in front of your friends if he wins once again. The resulting overdose of short-term Acute Stress can lead to psychological distress, tension and other physiological and emotional disorders.

The good news about short-term Acute Stress is that it is short lived and does not involve enough time to do the extensive damage associated with long-term stress.

The APA cites the most common symptoms related to short-term Acute Stress:

- Emotional distress, meaning some combination of anger/irritability, anxiety and depression, the three stress emotions.
- Muscular problems, including tension headaches, back pain, jaw pain and muscular tensions that lead

to pulled muscles and tendon and ligament problems.
- Stomach, gut and bowel problems, such as heartburn, acid stomach, flatulence, diarrhea, constipation and IBS.
- Transient over-arousal can lead to elevation in blood pressure, rapid heartbeat, sweaty palms, heart palpitations, dizziness, migraine headaches, cold hands or feet, shortness of breath and chest pain.

Most people experience some form of Acute Stress on a daily basis. It is quite manageable and very treatable.

Episodic Acute Stress

Those who suffer from Episodic Acute Stress frequently live their lives in a disordered, chaotic manner—in a state of perpetual crisis. They find themselves constantly in the grasp of Acute Stress, failing to manage their time efficiently and allowing self-inflicted demands to increase pressure and stress levels.

Typically, these individuals overreact to stimuli and become short-tempered, anxious and irritable. In many cases, they may not be able to express themselves without coming across as abrupt or hostile. Their work environment may become difficult to endure.

Type A personalities may suffer to a far greater degree, experiencing aggressive behavior, a higher level of impatience and compulsive competitiveness.

Episodic Acute Stress is exemplified by negative thinkers who worry incessantly about possible problems and catastrophes that may arise. They have a tendency to become anxious and depressed.

Their personality and lifestyle issues may be so deeply rooted and habitual that they believe this is their normal behavior pattern. They perceive their world as being a part of who they are and often blame their own distress on others or external events.

Some of the symptoms of Episodic Acute Stress are as follows:

- Persistent tension headaches or migraines
- Hypertension
- Chest pain and heart disease

Those who suffer from Episodic Acute Stress may relentlessly resist change and rely solely on the potential of relief from their pain and discomfort by placing their trust in a treatment or recovery program. Professional treatment may last many months or years.

Chronic Stress

The Mayo Clinic staff wrote an article titled "Chronic Stress Puts Your Health at Risk." They mention how you may face multiple demands each day, such as shouldering huge workloads, making ends meet and taking care of your family. You might consider these hassles as threats and feel that you are under constant assault.

When you encounter a perceived threat, such as your employment hours being cut back, an insulting boss, a difficult employee or a strained relationship, your hypothalamus (a small region in your brain) sets off an alarm system within your body.

Through a combination of nerve and hormonal signals, this system prompts your adrenal glands to release a surge of hormones, including adrenaline and cortisol.

Adrenaline increases your heart rate, elevates your blood pressure and increases your energy supplies. Cortisol, the primary stress hormone, boosts sugar levels in the bloodstream, enhances your brain's use of glucose and increases the availability of substances that repair tissues.

Cortisol also stifles bodily functions that are nonessential or detrimental in a fight-or-flight situation by altering immune system responses. It suppresses the digestive system, the reproductive system and growth processes. This natural alarm system is quite complex and communicates with regions of the brain that control mood, motivation and fear.

The body's self-regulating stress-response system returns hormone levels to normal once a perceived threat has passed. As adrenaline and cortisol levels drop, your heart rate and blood pressure return to normal functioning levels while other systems resume their regular activities.

The problem begins when stressors are always present, and one feels constantly under attack and in the fight-or-flight mode.

The overexposure to cortisol and other stress hormones can disrupt almost all of your body's processes when they are under a constant, long-term activation of the stress-response system.

According to the Mayo Clinic, this puts one at a greater risk of numerous health issues, including these:

- Anxiety
- Depression
- Digestive problems
- Heart disease
- Sleep problems
- Weight gain
- Memory and concentration impairment

Chronic Stress can debilitate and immobilize a person. This is the constant, eroding stress that wears people down over time. It weakens the mind, destroys the body and deteriorates life.

The overwhelming stress of despised jobs or careers, broken relationships or marriages, financial disasters or dysfunctional families can take its toll on Chronic Stress sufferers. Persistent troubles and misfortunes are the norm and lead to physical, emotional and mental instability.

For these individuals, hope is lost and they can foresee no way out of their miserable situation. They eventually succumb to the inevitably grim outcome of their lives.

Chronic Stress can originate from traumatic childhood experiences. These painful memories become internalized and remain hidden under the surface, affecting the course of the sufferer's life. Most people are not even aware that these issues are there, contributing to their chronic stress.

People are immediately aware of Acute Stress because it is new to them and present in their awareness. They ignore Chronic Stress because it is familiar and has been with them for many years, if not most of their lives.

Other symptoms of Chronic Stress are as follows:

- Suicidal thoughts and tendencies
- Violence
- Heart attacks
- Strokes

- Possibly cancer

Chronic Stress symptoms are typically very difficult to approach and require long-term treatment, including behavioral therapy (and stress management therapy.)

Using Stress to Your Advantage

It is most advantageous to recognize when you have encountered a stressful situation. As soon as you are aware that you are under stress, you can place your attention on the event or thoughts that are causing the stress.

Once you are fully aware of the stress trigger, you may then decide to use this stress to motivate yourself to create your desired outcome. I used the word "decide" because one can basically make a decision that determines how the trigger may be perceived.

If one decides that the stress is too difficult or more than one can bear then the stress may have a negative outcome.

For instance, let's say you have a report that is due tomorrow, and you have just begun to work on it. You waited until the last moment to compile your research and report your findings. You realize now that it is going to take much longer to complete than you anticipated.

Panic sets in, and you find yourself solidly in the grasp of a very stressful situation. Your fear is that you will not complete the task on time and that you will look like a fool when you are asked to make your presentation to your superiors.

This fear overcomes you, and you believe this situation may severely diminish your value with your employer and perhaps leave you searching for another job.

The stress is so great that it prohibits you from focusing on creating a professional-quality presentation. The thought of the fearful outcome consumes you and your time, and you fail at your task.

A slight shift in your awareness and focus can eliminate this disastrous situation. Suppose you recognize the stress trigger and decide to use it to your advantage in the following manner.

You view the project as one that you not only *need* to complete but *want* to complete. You make the decision that this event will be meaningful to you and your superiors and that you will find a way to make it happen on time while providing the very best quality possible.

You find motivation and inspiration for the desired results within you in a positive way. You use this situation to rise above the stress and inspire yourself to complete the endeavor with resolve and dedication.

Now you are in position to leverage your time and efforts to create the best presentation possible. You have placed yourself in a mindset of positive influence with the forecast of a favorable outcome.

Identifying the causes of stress in our lives is the most important step we can take to reduce or eliminate common stressors. Becoming aware of stressful situations and perhaps writing down the causes can lead to means of effectively dealing with them.

In the example above, you should identify the stressor as the fact that your report is due tomorrow, and you don't feel you have the time to get it done. You make a mental or written note of it and discover that your best option is to find ways to create more time during your day to compile your research.

You decide to shorten your lunch hour and eliminate as many interruptions as possible by hanging a "Please do not disturb" sign on your office door or by letting coworkers know that you cannot socialize today due to the importance of the report you must complete. You may even enlist the support and assistance of fellow employees with your project.

Once you recognize your stress trigger and become open to options for overcoming it, your mind will go about finding ways of achieving your goal. With the process of identifying your stress generator and acknowledging it, you have placed yourself in the driver's seat.

Awareness alone can make the difference in whether you move forward in a positive way or succumb to the pressure and fail. In most situations, awareness engenders a means to the desired outcome. All that is required at that point is taking action to initiate the process while maintaining an attitude of positive expectancy.

The outcomes of stressful situations and events in life boil down to the perspectives we choose to embrace. Life is as we choose it to be. Decide to make the very best of any situation regardless of possible outcomes. It is totally up to us to create positive results out of apparently stressful situations.

Thoughts about Labeling

There is no fundamental meaning to any event, occurrence or issue that takes place in one's life. The only meaning attached is the meaning one ascribes to it. These events are meaningless, they just occur. We assign meaning to them based on our individual belief systems and our perceptions.

Consider the hypothetical scenario of twin brothers, Jim and Jeb, who grew up in the same household. Their father was an abusive alcoholic who beat them and belittled them on a regular basis. Both twins were treated the same by their father until his death when the boys were 17 years of age.

Even though both boys were treated the same and lived in the same environment for all those years, they held opposing views of their life situations. Jim felt challenged by his father's oppressive behavior while Jeb felt defeated.

Jim graduated from a prestigious university with a law degree and is happily married with children. Jeb withdrew from society, became an alcoholic and never had children due to his fear of the possibility that he may turn out to be an abusive father as well.

Each of them viewed his situation from a different perspective. Each of them had the same opportunities and the same resources. However, they labeled the events in their lives differently based on their beliefs.

Jim believed that his father was making him strong and more determined to succeed in life while Jeb believed that his father was making him weak and fearful of life and thus causing him to fail. The contrasting paths the twins walked in life were a result of the beliefs each of them held.

As we believe, so shall we be!

Because of Jim's belief that his father's behavior made him strong, he labeled the events of his youth as stimulating, and he felt challenged to perform at his best in all things. Jeb believed that his treatment was crippling, and he labeled his childhood events as disastrous, which caused him to lose faith in himself and in life.

Once we have labeled an event in our minds and assigned meaning to it, the event produces feelings (or emotions). We may feel delighted, inspired and challenged or pressured, anxious and defeated. If we label an event as impossible or too difficult to approach, we may feel anxious or overwhelmed. If we label it just as it is, merely an event with possibilities, the negative charge is released and avenues for success will manifest themselves.

We can choose to label an event with a positive attribute or a neutral one. Any event or situation can be labeled as it is. For example, instead of Jeb labeling his past events as disastrous, he could label them without adjectives. He could say "My father was abusive, he beat me, he belittled me." Those are the facts. Those are the events.

There is no inherent meaning to any of the events that took place in his youth. As with many other events in life, they are just things that happened: like playing in a little league softball game, going to a movie or experiencing your first kiss.

A first kiss can be a warm, blissful feeling for one individual and a terrifying ordeal for another. Our beliefs will determine exactly how we experience our lives.

Of course, being abused by a parent would be an awful experience for anyone while it is actually happening. It is perfectly fine to feel the pain, anger, fear or any emotion that surfaces during any experience in life. We should acknowledge it, feel it fully and completely and then allow it to dissipate.

It is holding onto, reliving and fixating on unfavorable past experiences that keeps us in the grasp of negative emotions. Experiencing negative emotions over long periods of time can have a severe impact on our physical, mental and emotional well-being.

Our minds are constantly at work, labeling situations that arise in our day-to-day experience. Once we become accustomed to creating labels that are either neutral or positively meaningful, we will be able to experience less stress and move towards outcomes that are more conducive to our innermost desires.

By changing one's perception from a label of impossibility, i.e., "I'll never get this done in time," to a mindset of "What are my possibilities?" a new set of thoughts come into play. These thoughts become open and engaging and bring about solutions that may not have been considered by someone with a defeatist attitude.

Positivity can be a most important ally in times of pressure and immediacy. It switches the current in our brains from moving us toward disaster to moving us on a course of fulfillment.

All it takes is a slight shift in the way we think to bring about positive results. Everything that happens to us in life is influenced by our perception. We can place ourselves in a position of firm control of our lives when we understand the power of choice and learn to label our life's events the way we choose.

The events that we believe to generate the greatest stress in our lives can be reduced to inconsequential occurrences with the proper mindset.

Chapter Four

Reducing Stress

There are many ways of reducing stress in our lives. We'll cover some methods and techniques in this chapter that will help you make effective, lasting changes while reducing levels of stress. When common stressors can be reduced or eliminated, it frees us up to enjoy life to a far greater extent than we may have imagined.

Eliminating or reducing tension allows our minds to become clear and open to receiving information and answers to questions or concerns that we may have about our careers, family and social and spiritual environments.

We are far more likely to discover solutions to problems when our minds are still and uncluttered. A clear mind is in receiving mode and allows for information to flow easily and effortlessly. Difficult decisions are made with confidence and certainty when we are free from the distraction of undue stress.

When tension is released, life becomes more pleasurable. Our relationships with others are transformed, our state of mind is more stable and our physical health is improved.

Every area of our lives experiences improvement when we control our levels of stress. Work and play activities are enhanced and enjoyed at elevated levels. We perform better in our jobs when we are relaxed, and our creative expression is then amplified.

Our behavior is altered as a result, and we may find others recognizing the changes we are undergoing. Relationships are improved, new relationships are formed and we may even discover a newfound appreciation for ourselves.

My behavior is at its worst when I am mentally stressed. Mental tension finds its way into my muscles and bones, and I experience aches, pains and digestive issues. As soon as I recognize the symptoms of excess stress in my physical being, I am able to confront the causes with an arsenal of relaxation techniques that I have learned throughout the years.

Ideally, it would be best to remain in a relaxed state at all times, but life has its way of cluttering us up with busy schedules, catastrophes and interruptions to our natural flow. When things are flowing well and life is fun, it can be easy to withdraw from the techniques that serve to enhance our states of being.

Being consistent with meditation and relaxation practices is the key to enjoying an ongoing sense of fulfillment in our daily lives. The reason yoga, meditation and breathing techniques are referred to as "practices" is because they are skills that one must practice in order to become proficient with them.

Anything, whether it's a sport, hobby or behavioral adjustment, at which one desires to become skillful requires patience, diligence and practice. Dramatically improving the quality of our lives deserves complete attention and resolve in order to reap the desired benefits.

Meditation has been proven to reduce stress, which can help reduce or eliminate some or all symptoms of many diseases and conditions. However, if there are deep, unresolved emotional issues or beliefs that are interfering with your health, other types of therapy may be necessary.

Breathing

Proper breathing is paramount to a healthy mind and body. If your tendency is toward shallow breathing, as mine is, then it is even more important that you discover ways of bringing more oxygen into your body on a regular basis.

Being that the body is approximately two-thirds oxygen, it is vital that we optimize breathing techniques in order to aid in our metabolic processes. Oxygen provides energy, and proper breathing increases this energy while exercising the lungs and allowing them to eliminate carbon dioxide and other toxins from our systems.

Breathing correctly can not only increase energy but relax a person and allow their body to heal. It can reduce blood pressure, improve focus and concentration, eliminate toxins, strengthen the immune system, improve bowel function, reduce stress, tension and anxiety, increase feelings of calmness and relaxation and increase the metabolism while aiding in digestion and weight loss, along with many other benefits.

Without realizing it, people in pain (or not in pain) will often hold their breath for short periods of time. They will also frequently experience a very shallow disordered breathing pattern. While this is more than likely an unconscious, protective reaction to pain, it can actually increase the level of pain and worsen other symptoms.

Breathing incorrectly can cause problems in a number of bodily systems, including the immune, circulatory, endocrine and nervous systems. Improper breathing can produce various symptoms, including dizziness, chest pain, mental fog, anxiety, digestive issues, irritable bowels and head, neck and shoulder pain.

There are far too many breathing techniques to explore in this book, so I suggest that you research breath work in addition to the subsequent exercises in this chapter.

The first three exercises are suggested by Dr. Andrew Weil and may be found on his website.

1: The Stimulating Breath (also called the Bellows Breath)

The Stimulating Breath is adapted from a yogic breathing technique. Its aim is to raise vital energy and increase alertness.

- *Inhale and exhale rapidly through your nose, keeping your mouth closed but relaxed. Your breaths in and out should be equal in duration and as short as possible. This is a noisy breathing exercise.*

- *Try for three in-and-out breath cycles per second. This produces a quick movement of the diaphragm, suggesting a bellows. Breathe normally after each cycle.*
- *Do not perform this exercise for more than 15 seconds on your first try. Each time you practice the Stimulating Breath, you can increase your time by five seconds or so, until you reach a full minute.*

If done properly, you may feel invigorated; it should be comparable to the heightened awareness you feel after a good workout. You should feel the effort at the back of the neck, the diaphragm, the chest and the abdomen. Try this breathing exercise the next time you need an energy boost and feel yourself reaching for a cup of coffee.

2: The 4-7-8 (or Relaxing Breath)

This exercise is utterly simple, takes almost no time, requires no equipment and can be done anywhere. Although you can do the exercise in any position, sit with your back straight while learning the exercise.

Place the tip of your tongue against the ridge of tissue just behind your upper front teeth, and keep it there through the entire exercise. You will be exhaling through your mouth around your tongue; try pursing your lips slightly if this seems awkward.

- *Exhale completely through your mouth, making a "whoosh" sound.*
- *Close your mouth and inhale quietly through your nose to a mental count of **four**.*
- *Hold your breath for a count of **seven**.*
- *Exhale completely through your mouth, making a whoosh sound to a count of **eight**.*
- *This is one breath. Now inhale again and repeat the cycle three more times for a total of four breaths.*

Note that you always inhale quietly through your nose and exhale audibly through your mouth. The tip of your tongue stays in position the whole time. Exhalation takes twice as long as inhalation. The absolute time you spend on each phase is not important; the ratio of 4:7:8 is important. If you have trouble holding your breath, speed the exercise up but keep to the ratio of 4:7:8 for the three phases. With practice, you can slow it all down and get used to inhaling and exhaling more and more deeply.

This exercise is a natural tranquilizer for the nervous system. Unlike tranquilizing drugs, which are often effective when you first take them but then lose their power over time, this exercise is subtle when you first try it but gains in power with repetition and practice. Do it at least twice a day. You cannot do it too frequently. Do not try more than four breaths at one time for the first month of practice. Later, if you wish, you can extend it to eight breaths. If you feel a little lightheaded when you first breathe this way, do not be concerned, it will pass.

Once you develop this technique by practicing it every day, it will be a very useful tool that you will always have with you. Use it whenever anything upsetting happens—before you react. Use it whenever you are aware of internal tension. Use it to help you fall asleep. This exercise cannot be recommended too highly. Everyone can benefit from it.

3: Breath Counting

If you want to get a feel for this challenging work, try your hand at breath counting, a deceptively simple technique much used in Zen practice.

Sit in a comfortable position with the spine straight and head inclined slightly forward. Gently close your eyes and take a few deep breaths. Then let the breath come naturally without trying to influence it. Ideally it will be quiet and slow, but depth and rhythm may vary.

- *To begin the exercise, count "one" to yourself as you exhale.*
- *The next time you exhale, count "two," and so on up to "five."*
- *Then begin a new cycle, counting "one" on the next exhalation.*

Never count higher than "five," and count only when you exhale. You will know your attention has wandered (from your breath) when you find yourself up to "eight," "12" or even "19."
Try to do 10 minutes of this form of meditation.
Now for some other breathing exercises.

4: Abdominal Breathing

Place one hand on the abdomen (belly) and the other on the chest. Take a long, deep breath through the nose and ensure the diaphragm is in motion and not the chest. Inflate and stretch the lungs while expanding the diaphragm. Take six or eight slow breaths per minute for about 10 minutes each day. You may experience immediate reductions in your heart rate and blood pressure. This exercise is especially beneficial when used prior to an exam, job assignment or any stressful event.

5: Progressive Relaxation

Sit comfortably in a chair with feet flat on the floor. The focus will be on tensing muscle groups, beginning with the feet and ankles, calves, thighs, buttocks, chest, arms, hands, shoulders, neck and jaw and finishing with the eyes. Breathe long and slow in through the nose, a full breath into the diaphragm, and then hold the breath while tensing one muscle group at a time to the count of three. Then relax the muscles while exhaling through the mouth. Begin with the feet and ankles and move your way up the body, focusing on one muscle group per breath.

This is a great way to relax the entire body and is great to do in the evening before bedtime. If you become lightheaded or dizzy, ease off a bit and hold the breath for just a second or two. You may build up to holding for five seconds when you feel comfortable.

6: One-Minute Breathing to Relax

Inhale to the count of two
Exhale to the count of two
Inhale to the count of two
Exhale to the count of three
Inhale to the count of two
Exhale to the count of four
Inhale to the count of two
Exhale to the count of five
Repeat this several times and notice your increased level of relaxation along with a sharper focus. This is helpful to stay on task while stimulating the creative energy within you.

7: Lion's Breath

Lion's Breath relieves tension in the face by stretching the jaw and tongue. Once learned, it can be done in almost any pose.

1. Come to kneel with your buttocks resting on your feet.
2. Place your hands on your thighs.
3. Inhale through the nose.
4. Exhale through the mouth, making a "ha" sound. As you exhale, open your mouth wide and stick your tongue as far out as possible towards your chin.
5. Inhale while returning to a neutral face.
6. Repeat 3–5 times.

There are many great sources on the internet, including YouTube, that can provide instant information and instruction. Also, participating with a local yoga or other health group or organization can contribute to your well-being.

Yoga

Yoga can be described as the purpose of uniting the mind, body and spirit. It involves creating balance in the body through developing both strength and flexibility. This is done through the performance of poses or postures which have specific mental and physical benefits.

There are many styles of yoga which approach breathing, postures and philosophy in a variety of means. You do not have to be physically flexible or strong to practice yoga. You can easily find a style that is suited for your physical and spiritual needs.

Many of the breathing exercises today have evolved from yogic practice and have endured a thousand years or more. Yoga works to instill an awareness of self and causes us to move beyond our physical limitations. It helps us tap into deeper and more subtle levels of awareness.

There are various paths of yoga that are a part of a comprehensive system. Some of these specialized branches are Hatha, Karma, Mantra, Bhakti, Jnana and Raja. One must not feel the need to undertake a specific path such as these.

Very simple, basic yoga techniques can be learned without the need to become involved with any particular style at a deep level. Local YMCAs and civic organizations offer basic yoga classes that will fulfill the needs of anyone looking to reduce stress and learn breathing techniques to improve health.

Do a little research, find a yoga class, check out yoga DVDs at a local library or visit YouTube for instant instruction. Yoga is a fine way to reduce stress, become physically fit and develop a deeper sense of awareness for living a more fulfilled life.

Exercise

The importance of exercise cannot be over-emphasized. There are so many immediate and long-term benefits to fitness. Our lives can be transformed in many areas as a result of an ongoing exercise routine.

A multitude of exercise routines are available. They encompass a variety of methods and styles to suit anyone's needs. Once we realize the importance of the role that regular exercise plays in our lives and the value it presents to us, we must opt in and learn to enjoy its benefits.

Exercise can help us look better, feel better, have more energy and perhaps even help us live longer. It can perk up our sex lives, better our moods, enhance our performance in the workplace and provide opportunities for more joy in our lives. Other tremendous benefits include weight control and improved sleeping habits.

The Mayo Clinic cites exercise as being responsible for increasing HDL (good cholesterol) while decreasing unhealthy triglycerides. It increases blood flow, which decreases the risk of cardiovascular disease. The Mayo Clinic also states that regular physical activity can help prevent or manage a wide range of health problems and concerns, including stroke, metabolic syndrome, type 2 diabetes, depression, certain types of cancer and arthritis.

When implementing your exercise program, create realistic goals. Make them easy to attain in the beginning, and then work yourself up to a greater level of conditioning. Once you are able to recognize the positive changes occurring in your physical, emotional and mental well-being, a new sense of satisfaction and accomplishment will aid in taking you the distance.

According to the American College of Sports Medicine, more than half of new exercisers quit within three to six months of starting an exercise program. Being proactive and planning ahead for interruptions to your schedule can help you adhere to your workout intentions. Whatever you do, don't get discouraged. Stay the course.

Make sure you are in a good position to engage in an exercise routine. Check with your medical practitioner before beginning your program to be certain your health is in order for the routine you have chosen.

Walking: It's one of the easiest, most healthful exercises you can do. It can be done almost anywhere: in the office, in your neighborhood, at the gym on a treadmill, at a park or in a shopping mall. You can begin with five or ten minutes and work your way up to an ideal 30 minutes or more. You can quicken your pace, add inclines or even walk backwards at times. Be sure you have a good pair of walking shoes.

Interval Training: Boost your fitness level with interval training, which burns more calories. Varying the intensity of your workout instead of going at a steady pace is the ideal. You can walk, jog, dance, do pushups or a variety of other cardiovascular exercises. Switch things up and change your routine often to make it interesting. A trainer can assist in developing a program that best suits your needs.

Swimming: It is probably the best low-impact exercise available. The impact of the ground is eliminated, so your joints are more protected from stress and strain. The Arthritis Foundation recommends swimming and *other water activities for this very reason. Swimming improves endurance, strength, muscle tone and can even build muscle mass. It also burns an incredible amount of calories and can be very relaxing, refreshing and fun.*

Dance: There are many types of dance routines to meet the needs of just about anyone. Zumba is very popular and can be quite a workout. Jazzercise, Hip Hop, Belly Dancing, Salsa, Ballroom, Ballet and scores of others are available to make your exercise routine exciting and social as well.

Find an exercise program that appeals to you, whether it is low-impact swimming or high-energy martial arts. Set a goal and make it happen. Get started today!

Diet

We all understand the importance of exercise. Exercising while consuming a poor, imbalanced diet high in sugars and fats and low in fiber will do little to improve our state of health. It is the well-rounded approach of good exercise in combination with a healthy diet that is most effective.

Changing a diet can be a challenge if you have certain health issues that restrict important foods or food groups. Food allergies, blood types and other factors may necessitate acquiring a doctor's recommendation or a nutritionist's expertise.

Consult your doctor or health practitioner for advice that is specific to your needs. A cohesive plan of action must be implemented for optimum results.

Meditation

Meditation is at the center of the wheel of good health. It is the hub that joins the spokes of breathing, exercise, diet, relaxation, energy and awareness together.

The next chapter is dedicated to meditation and the techniques that may enhance all areas of your health.

Chapter Five

Meditation

In May of 2015, *The Washington Post* published an article about a Harvard Medical School neuroscientist, Sara Lazar Ph.D., who is also with the Massachusetts General Hospital. Dr. Lazar challenged the claims about the benefits of meditation and mindfulness and tested them with brain scans.

In her studies, she found that meditating can literally change the brain. With her initial research, she discovered evidence that meditation was associated with decreased stress, decreased depression, anxiety, pain and insomnia while providing an increase in the quality of life.

Her studies displayed that meditators had more gray matter in various areas of the brain, including the frontal cortex, which is associated with working memory and executive decision making.

Her staff took people who had never meditated before through an eight-week mindfulness-based stress reduction program (MBSR) and revealed amazing results.

They found differences in brain volume in five different regions in the participants' brains after only eight weeks. Four areas of their brains *increased* in volume. These areas are responsible for self-relevance, learning cognition, memory, emotional regulation, perspective taking, empathy and compassion. Also, the area in the brain stem where regulatory neurotransmitters are produced showed an increase.

The fifth area, the amygdala, showed a *decrease* in volume. The amygdala is responsible for the fight-or-flight part of the brain, which is important for producing feelings of anxiety, fear and stress in general. This change correlated in a positive way to reduced stress levels *(The Washington Post, May 26, 2015)*.

Meditation has a variety of meanings depending on who you ask. Some feel that meditation is strictly a means for relaxation or an opportunity to sit in quiet contemplation. Others believe that there is a higher, spiritual element to the practice. There are many reasons to meditate and as many types of meditation to respond to an individual's needs and desires.

True meditation may not be about relaxation, contemplation or concentration. It may merely be a state of non-cognition or thoughtless awareness. The term "pure beingness" describes the experience in which one meditates in the truest sense of the word.

Meditation may be most effective when we are in a state of thoughtless awareness. There is no need to do anything. It is in the non-doing that the mind becomes still and the body relaxes. We are aware of thoughts that enter our mind, and we allow them to drift by in a similar way to watching a leaf in a stream float by and disappear into the forest.

Of course, there are many kinds of meditation, and each of them has different goals and means to achieve various states of being. Find a practice that is best suited to your inclinations.

Types of Meditation

Traditionally, meditation was held within the context of spiritual or religious beliefs, teachings and practices. The objective was to transform everyday consciousness into a state of receptiveness regarding the goals of the tradition. It dates back thousands of years. Variations include sitting, standing, lying down and walking. Eyes may be open and unfocused or, more commonly, closed.

Some types of meditation may be performed in a state of mind involving awareness and acceptance and can be done at almost any time while in the midst of any activity. Certain styles may be more difficult to learn than others, and most fall into one of several general categories.

Concentrative or Focused Meditation. This practice involves placing the attention on something specific, such as a phrase repeated in the mind (a mantra), the breath, a sound or an image. The training consists of repeatedly returning to the focal point and helps an individual develop the capacity to remain calm and grounded. Overcoming distractions and sustaining mental focus through the power of concentration helps quiet the mind. One can learn to harness the power of the mind by developing the energies of concentration and focus. A scattered, fragmentary flow of attention can be disciplined into a distraction-free, extraordinary state of being that is conducive to higher learning capabilities, calmness and intuitive guidance.

Open Awareness Meditation: These styles of meditative practices concentrate on opening the mind into an expansive awareness of surroundings without a specific focus. The ability to be present with whatever comes to mind, without judging it, is developed through this practice. Unlike focused meditation, open awareness can be compared to using our consciousness from a wide angle or panoramic viewpoint. One learns to be present and observe without the use of concentration or guidance.

There is no effort to direct the focus toward any object, only a relaxed awareness. The Tibetan Buddhist practice of Dzogchen uses meditation in this manner.

Mindfulness Meditation: This traditional Buddhist style is the most popular and the most researched meditation practice in the Western world. It can be somewhat of a combination of concentration and open awareness. It is most commonly identified with the Buddhist practice of Vipassana or "insight" meditation, but it may be found in various contemplative traditions. The focus is usually directed to the breath. This allows the wandering, busy mind a place of refuge by bringing it back to a solitary focal point. The practitioner does not concentrate on the breath. It is more about bringing the active mind back to the present moment, where the breath resides. This practice is often extended to daily activities, such as eating, bathing, exercising and job-related tasks.

Guided Meditation: Many forms of meditation incorporate guided meditation into their practice. These may be delivered in person or via audio or video recording. In them, the recipient uses imagery or affirmations to guide themselves into various states of being or just back to the present moment. Guided imagery has become very popular and is used to facilitate good health and well-being. It is used to promote healing after surgeries and enhance athletic performance, and it has a wide array of business and personal applications as well.

One may need to experiment with several types of meditation in order to find a style that meets their needs and expectations.

I enjoy utilizing a number of meditative styles depending on my current situation, but it may be more effective if one chooses a style and sticks with it for a while until they become totally comfortable with it.

Once a person becomes proficient with their practice, they may be able to expand their interests and find other meditative styles to be effective as well. Trying to learn several types of meditation at one time may become overwhelming and counterproductive.

We all progress at our own pace. Some may learn techniques quickly and develop their practice at deeper levels than others. There is no specific time frame for developing a practice. Enter into it with a willing heart and an open mind, and the practice will expand with the timing and effectiveness determined by each individual's intentions and willingness to learn.

One person may find the results they are looking for within weeks, and another may discover that it will be months before they recognize a shift in their well-being. However, even if one does not see evidence of positive change, their practice will be providing benefits anyway.

There are subtle changes that will take place without conscious recognition most of the time. Continuing the practice on a regular schedule will be effective and will provide long-term results regardless of how one may perceive it. Repetition develops skill, and practicing a meditative technique daily will produce positive results.

One must be patient and enter into meditation without expecting immediate results. In fact, there should be no expectations at all. Meditation is about being, not doing or expecting.

Positive expectations are great in life, and we should remain positive as much as possible, but during meditation, the mind should be free from goals and desires. This is a time to quiet the mind and allow the process to unfold as it will.

When we expect certain things to happen during meditation and nothing appears to happen, we set ourselves up for disappointment and discouragement. There is nothing that "should" happen during meditation except a free and clear mind and a relaxed body. The mind and body will relax and respond on levels that may not be recognized immediately.

Of course, guided meditations are different in that they direct the mind to create situations and feelings that should be experienced vividly during that time. This is the exception with a guided imagery style of meditative practice.

Let's now explore several popular meditation styles and techniques.

Transcendental Meditation or TM: Transcendental Meditation was introduced to the western world by Maharishi Mahesh Yogi in the 1950s. It is a simple technique that is generally practiced twice per day for 20 minutes each session. The practitioner sits comfortably with the eyes closed and repeats a mantra that is given to them by a certified TM teacher.

This practice requires the personalized attention of a TM instructor to get started. There is a fee involved for learning the technique that may be upwards of a thousand dollars. The TM practice does not involve concentration or control of the mind. There is no contemplation or monitoring of thoughts involved.

This easy-to-learn process allows the active mind to quiet down to a state of inner calm and can be learned by anyone of any age, religion or culture. It is not a religion, philosophy or lifestyle, and it is practiced by over six million people worldwide.

It allows one's mind to experience quieter levels of thought until a peaceful awareness or pure consciousness is obtained. TM refers to this as *automatic self-transcending.*

Zazen: This can be described, in Buddhism, as the study of self and has been practiced for over two thousand years. Zazen is a very easy, simple Zen (school of Buddhism) practice that produces the best results when consistently engaged. Particular attention is paid to the positioning of the body. The seated position is the ideal in this tradition, which has an impact on the breath as well as the mind. Zazen views the body, breath and mind as one reality.

For this practice, a symmetrical position is preferred, using a small pillow under the buttocks with the knees touching the ground, forming somewhat of a tripod base that is stable and grounded. Most importantly, the spine should be straight and in line with the neck and head. The eyes may be closed or open slightly, with the hands relaxed over the belly, one hand cupped in the other, and the tips of the thumbs touching to form somewhat of a circle.

There are several seated positions utilized with traditional Zazen. They range from the cross-legged Burmese, half Lotus and full Lotus to kneeling or chair positions. These positions contribute to the straightening of the spine, allowing the diaphragm to move more freely, providing for deeper breathing. The breath is a focal point as it is the vital force and a major central activity of the body.

Zazen breath work starts with the counting of breaths. The process begins with the mouth closed, breathing through the nose, counting "one" for the first inhale, "two" for the first exhale and then continuing to the count of ten.

This exercise is repeated until the mind begins to quiet down. Each time the mind wanders during the process, the practitioner becomes aware of the thoughts, acknowledges them and then allows them to fade away by returning the focus to the counting of breaths.

Once the individual is comfortable with the practice and the mind has become consistently quiet during these times, the next level of counting should be performed.

Each breathing cycle is now experienced as the combination of an inhale followed by an exhale, ending with the count of "one." The next inhale and exhale cycle is at the count of "two" and so forth.

At some point, the need for counting breaths will dissipate, and the focus will then be on the breathing itself. Eventually, the mind will quiet, and there will be no need for counting or paying attention to the breath.

Of course, this entire process may need to be repeated each time one settles in for meditation. Some will reach a quieter level of mind much quicker than others. As with all meditation styles, the more often it is practiced, the greater the results that will be achieved.

Dzogchen: Pronounced *zoke-chen,* which means "the Great Perfection" in Tibetan. This Buddhist style of meditation is known as non-meditation due to its lack of attention to a mantra, to the breath or to any other thing. It is about non-focus, non-doing and just being.

Dzogchen's emphasis is on spontaneity, openness, authenticity, joy and lightness. It is preferred that one learns the processes through a traditional teacher of Dzogchen as there are many deeper levels of the practice involving sitting, chanting, self-inquiry and attitude transformation.

The everyday practice of Dzogchen is about developing a complete acceptance and openness to all situations without limitations. It's about experiencing everything without resistance or judgements. One releases fixed attentions and allows life to unfold just as it is.

The practitioner sits quietly, without the urge to delve into the mind or withdraw from the world. The practice is free, non-conceptual and without introspection or concentration.

Dzogchen posits that the Buddha is within each of us and that we are all enlightened already. We just need to realize this and live our lives as if we are the embodiment of unconditional love, peace and understanding. We are to be this rather than attempting to attain it.

Guided Meditation: Guided meditation is very popular, and I enjoy it from time to time, depending on my personal needs. I prefer silent meditation and believe that its benefits are greater to me in the long run than those from guided meditations. However, guided meditations produce excellent results for specific issues.

For instance, if I am struggling with an intense work schedule that is compromising my ability to relax and complete my personal activities then I may elect to engage in a guided meditation specifically designed for mental and physical relaxation.

Also, I may have a physical issue that requires attention, such as a sore back or a headache. There are specific guided imagery meditations available that are directed toward relaxing muscles and increasing oxygen levels to promote healing.

There are times when I want to increase my awareness of the energy flowing through the energy systems of my body and to balance these systems. One can easily find audio files or videos to help accomplish this. At other times, I'll have specific work-related goals to which I want to bring more attention, so I will seek out an appropriate recording.

These, and many other guided meditations, may be found on YouTube and other sources online. Meditation videos for IBS, ulcerative colitis and Crohn's disease may be discovered, too. These videos can be beneficial for those who suffer from these syndromes, or just about any other health issue, and can be used to supplement an ongoing meditation practice.

You can find meditations for insomnia, anxiety, diet, personal conflict and relationships, energy, mental and physical health, sales and employment, relaxation or deep meditation. Other areas of focus include achieving goals, family, happiness and joy and overcoming obstacles such as fear, procrastination and traumatic experiences.

Guided meditations may be in the form of print, audio or video and can result in benefits that may be realized instantly or over a period of time.

One great benefit to these types of meditations is that they are instantly available at no cost. One must be careful that the provider is honorable and knowledgeable in the area of the request. Be mindful and do some research on the background of the provider before committing to the meditation.

Guided meditations can be fun, enjoyable, relaxing, educational, healing and spiritually satisfying. Experiment with various kinds and discover how they can benefit your life by providing an easy, meaningful way of journeying toward good health and happiness.

The Silva Method: Jose Silva created this worldwide phenomenon back in the sixties, and millions of people now use his techniques. He used a somewhat scientific approach and developed a system that is not only simple but extremely effective.

The Silva Method is now part of the Mindvalley company. I have used Jose's system for around 20 years and have found it produces amazing results. His *"Three, Two, One Method"* is easy for anyone to learn and is quite ingenious.

This simple system is designed to train the individual to gain control of the mind so that it can be used to its fullest potential. The Three, Two, One Method trains the mind to relax the body at Level Three. Then it teaches the mind to relax at Level Two. After this, one can attain the Alpha state, at Level One, more easily.

First, the individual takes a deep breath and exhales while mentally reciting the number "three" three times and visualizing the number "three" at each count during this one breath.

This is Level Three, where the physical body experiences relaxation. The practitioner then takes a couple of moments to relax each section of the body, beginning with the head and moving down to the toes.

Next, the individual takes a deep breath and exhales while mentally reciting the number "two" three times and visualizing the number "two" at each count.

Level Two is where the mind learns to relax and becomes quiet. A familiar, comforting, relaxing scene is brought to mind and experienced in vivid detail, inducing a state of mind that is relaxed and quiet.

Then the practitioner takes another deep breath and exhales while mentally reciting the number "one" three times and visualizing the number "one" at each count.

The individual is now at Level One, the Alpha level: a quieter, healthier state of mind. Alpha brain waves are present and can be achieved during light meditation. It is the optimal level for programming your mind for better health and success. The Alpha state sharpens your intuition, memory, visualization, imagination, learning and concentration. It lies at the base of your conscious awareness and is the gateway to your subconscious mind.

The beauty of this process is that, as you practice the technique repeatedly, each level becomes easier and quicker to achieve. At first, it may take five to ten minutes to reach the Alpha state. Then, over a period of time, one may be able to breeze right through the levels to the Alpha state in just a moment due to the established reference points created during the process.

A practitioner may even begin to feel the effects of Alpha brain waves as soon as they start counting the first set of number three. They will have learned to control the mind and use it as a tool to produce the results they desire.

I use this technique to begin most of my meditations, and then I can continue on by choosing among any number of other styles of meditation. However, most styles of meditation do not require one to achieve the Alpha state in order to enter into meditation. Deeper levels of consciousness may be obtained with any meditative technique and are a result of quieting the mind and body.

Of course, the Silva Method teaches deepening techniques that are quite effective as well. There are also many other programs within the Silva Life System that may appeal to you.

Mindfulness Meditation: Also known as Vipassana or Insight Meditation, this style is based on a 25-hundred-year-old tradition that is non-sectarian and non-religious. It is one of the most popular styles of meditation in the world. This path consists of self-transformation through self-observation and focuses on the deep interconnection between the mind and the body.

Cultivating mindfulness in our everyday experience of life is paramount in overcoming suffering and pain. Mindfulness is nurtured through the daily practice of meditation, which may be performed via formal sitting, relaxed walking or lying down, eating or with any activity, be it personal or business-related.

Mindfulness is not directed toward changing the way we are but about helping us become aware of what is already true and real about ourselves. It teaches us to be unconditionally present, accepting and non-judgmental with whatever life is offering us at the time.

Each of us is endowed with mindfulness, and this quality can be cultivated through meditation. Mindfulness is not thinking but an awareness of thinking and an awareness of how we experience our internal and external sensory worlds.

Mindfulness invites whatever arises in our awareness and is open-hearted and non-judgmental. It seeks to make us more aware of our moment-to-moment attention and asks us to be more present within our lives.

With a continuing practice, life will become characterized by an increased peaceful awareness and an elevated sense of allowing along with a confident feeling of self-control. Positive results will appear gradually as one progresses along the path.

Mindfulness meditation uses the seated position as do many other meditation traditions. The optimal position of choice for mindfulness meditation is seated, cross-legged with the buttocks on a pillow and the knees touching the floor. The back is straight, in a natural position in line with the neck and head. This allows easier, more complete breathing.

However, one may choose to sit upright in a chair with hands faced down on the thighs in a relaxed manner. Don't get too caught up with the formality. There are other facets to this style that one will learn as they proceed with the tradition.

Generally, the focus is on the breath: breathing in and out slowly and naturally, without forcing the mind's attention onto the breath. It's more about gently guiding the attention back to the breath as the mind wanders. One becomes aware of the thoughts, acknowledges them and then allows them to drift on by, returning to the breath each time a thought enters.

There are far deeper levels of the practice, depending on the school of instruction, that one may learn as they progress. However, a practitioner may stick with the basic meditation routine for as long as they wish.

This chapter has been dedicated to introducing you to meditation and providing basic information about some of the techniques. There are many other styles available; do some research and find one that interests you. You may end up experimenting with a couple of styles before you discover a good match.

Vishen Lakhiani, entrepreneur, education technology innovator, speaker, philanthropist and founder/CEO of Mindvalley, which specializes in personal development, recently interviewed Ken Wilber for one of Vishen's programs.

Ken Wilber is one of the most important philosophers in the world today. He is the most widely translated academic writer in America, with over 25 books, and his writings have been translated into 30 languages.

Vishen asked Ken, a veteran meditator, what he thought was the best, most powerful form of mediation available, and Ken replied, "Mindfulness."

He suggested practicing 20–30 minutes once or twice a day for a month or two and then, if this form of meditation seemed right for the individual, to research available mindfulness-based programs.

There are many support groups and organizations that utilize various meditation techniques which are easy to learn and quite effective. Seek out a local group that you can try out or join. Personal interaction and participation may have wonderful rewards. You can learn a great deal from others' mistakes and successes.

The next chapter will introduce you to Jon Kabat-Zinn's mindfulness meditation programs. As I mentioned earlier in this book, these programs have been the most influential for me and have created a powerful means of positive change and healing during the most challenging health issues of my life.

Chapter Six

A Path to a Healthy Mind and Body

Jon Kabat-Zinn is a most remarkable human being. He has given tens of thousands of suffering people ways of eliminating or reducing pain, illness and stress in their lives. Jon is a master of the techniques he teaches and is the leader in the field of healing and stress reduction through mindfulness.

His many books and programs serve to foster positive change in the lives of those in need. The kind and caring ways in which he shares his processes and techniques is a testament to his devotion to serving humanity. He is patient and empathetic to the needs of all and demonstrates unconditional love and compassion through the work he performs.

I mentioned Jon and his work in the beginning of this book, and now I would like to formally introduce him to you.

Jon Kabat-Zinn, Ph.D. is a scientist, author and teacher of meditation. He is internationally known for his work in bringing mindfulness into mainstream healthcare, medicine and society.

He is an Emeritus Professor of Medicine at the University of Massachusetts Medical School, where he founded the school's world-renowned mindfulness-based Stress Reduction Clinic in 1979. He also founded the Center for Mindfulness in Medicine, Health Care and Society in 1995.

He has authored two best-selling books: *Full Catastrophe Living: Using the Wisdom of Your Body and Mind to Face Stress, Pain and Illness* and *Wherever You Go, There You Are: Mindfulness Meditation in Everyday Life.* In addition to these, he has written *Everyday Blessings: The Inner Work of Mindful Parenting* (co-authored with his wife Myla); *Coming to Our Senses: Healing Ourselves and the World through Mindfulness; The Mindful Way through Depression: Freeing Yourself from Chronic Unhappiness; Arriving at Your Own Door; Letting*

Everything Become Your Teacher and *Mindfulness for Beginners*.

He was co-editor of two books, *The Mind's Own Physician: A Scientific Dialogue with the Dalai Lama on the Healing Power of Meditation* (with Richard Davidson) and *Mindfulness: Diverse Perspectives on its Meaning, Origins, and Applications* (with Mark Williams).

His common sense books and meditation programs are very relevant to today's lifestyles and have thoroughly changed the lives of thousands of people worldwide. His work has contributed greatly by integrating mindfulness into mainstream society, including medicine, health care and hospitals, schools, higher education, corporations, prisons, the legal profession and professional sports.

Dr. Kabat-Zinn received his Ph.D. in molecular biology from MIT in 1971 under the guidance of Nobel Laureate in physiology and medicine, Salvador Luria.

The research that Dr. Kabat-Zinn performed between 1979 and 2002 focused on mind-body interactions for healing, on various clinical applications of mindfulness meditation training for people with chronic pain and/or stress-related disorders, on the effects of MBSR on the brain and how it processes emotions, particularly under stress, and on the immune system.

His work in the Stress Reduction Clinic was featured in Bill Moyers' PBS Special, *Healing and the Mind* and also in the book with the same title.

Throughout his career, Dr. Kabat-Zinn has trained groups of judges, CEOs and business leaders, lawyers, clergy, and Olympic athletes (the 1984 Olympic Men's Rowing Team) in mindfulness. Over 720 medical centers and clinics nationwide and abroad now use his MBSR model.

In 1994, Dr. Kabat-Zinn received both the Interface Foundation Career Achievement Award and the New York Open Center's Tenth Year Anniversary Achievement in Medicine and Health Award. In 1998, he received the Art, Science, and Soul of Healing

Award from the Institute for Health and Healing at the California Pacific Medical Center in San Francisco, and in 2001, he received the second annual Trailblazer Award for "pioneering work in the field of integrative medicine" from the Scripps Center for Integrative Medicine in La Jolla, California.

In 2007, he received an Inaugural Pioneer in Integrative Medicine Award from the Bravewell Philanthropic Collaborative for Integrative Medicine, and the next year, the 2008 Mind and Brain Prize from the Center for Cognitive Science at the University of Turin, Italy. He is a founding fellow of the Fetzer Institute, a fellow of the Society of Behavioral Medicine and the founding convener of the Consortium of Academic Health Centers for Integrative Medicine, a network of deans, chancellors and faculty at major US medical schools engaged at the creative edges of mind-body and integrative medicine.

Dr. Kabat-Zinn also serves on the Board of the Mind and Life Institute, a group that organizes dialogues between the Dalai Lama and Western scientists and scholars to promote deeper understanding and harnessing for beneficial purposes different ways of knowing and probing the nature of the mind, emotions and reality. He was co-program chair of the 2005 Mind and Life Dialogue XIII: The Science and Clinical Applications of Meditation, held in Washington, DC.

The Programs

Mindfulness Meditation Series: Series 1, Series 2 and Series 3 were developed and voiced by Dr. Kabat-Zinn. These guided CDs are used by thousands of people who have participated in Dr. Kabat-Zinn's MBSR classes in the Stress Reduction Clinic at the University of Massachusetts Medical Center.

It is not necessary to visit the University of Massachusetts to derive benefits from this program. The series of CDs are designed to be used independently of the Medical Center's program and may be utilized in conjunction with Dr. Kabat-Zinn's books, *Full Catastrophe Living (2nd edition)*,

Wherever You Go, There You Are and *Coming to Our Senses.*

Each of these books corresponds to the CDs for Series 1, Series 2 and Series 3, respectively. These CDs are extremely effective in developing and deepening a personal mindfulness meditation practice. They can amount to a most liberating and healing experience for the person who indulges in the guided meditations.

The regular use of these CDs can provide an experience of stillness, well-being, clarity, wisdom and compassion. You will find this series of guided meditation CDs or digital downloads at **www.mindfulnesscds.com.**

MBSR Online Course via Sounds True: The Center for Mindfulness has partnered with Sounds True to provide the eight-week MBSR course as a self-guided video course.

Dr. Saki Santorelli, director of the Center for Mindfulness, and senior instructor Florence Meleo-

Meyer, director of the Oasis Institute for Mindfulness, co-authored the program. The course offers the same curriculum and methodology originally developed by Dr. Jon Kabat-Zinn and taught at the Center for Mindfulness in Medicine, Health Care and Society at the University of Massachusetts Medical School.

The course schedule consists of eight weekly classes and one day-long class. This highly participatory, practical course, presented by Dr. Saki Santorelli and Florence Meleo-Meyer, includes the following:

- More than 16 hours of video instruction on mindfulness meditation, stretching, mindful yoga and guidance for enhancing awareness in everyday life
- Four hours of guided mindfulness practice in audio form
- Elements from the in-person MBSR course workbook available in PDF format
- An online journal in which to record and reflect on your experiences
- A completion graph to track your progress through the course

- Two annual live sessions—"A Day in Mindfulness"
- Continuing practice emails, sent once a week for four weeks after you complete the course

All participants will also receive two free gifts:

- Discount of $50 off a purchase of $95 or more of selected mindfulness-based learning resources from Sounds True
- Free audio practice on kindness, presented by Florence Meleo-Meyer

The MBSR Online Course brings you the complete intensive training in mindfulness meditation and its integration into the challenges and adventures of everyday life. All materials in this course will be yours to keep—you can return to any previous session at any time to refresh your experience. You can find this course and other information at www.soundstrue.com.

MBSR 8-Week: This eight-week-long program is designed to empower the practitioner with tools that will aid in maximizing life when facing stress, illness and pain. During the program, you will be deliberately and systematically working with your own stress, illness or pain and the challenges of your everyday life.

Your instructors will create a safe and supportive environment for this work and learning through the following means:

• Guided instruction in mindfulness meditation practices
• Gentle stretching and mindful yoga
• Group dialogue and discussions aimed at enhancing awareness in everyday life
• Individually tailored instruction
• Daily home assignments
• Four home practice CDs and a home practice workbook

You will attend group classes for 2½ hours once a week for eight weeks. Classes are offered in the morning or evening. You receive 31 hours of direct instruction.
You will also attend one all-day weekend class in between classes 6 and 7.

The eight-week program is offered four times each year: in fall, winter, spring and summer. Classes are offered at the University of Massachusetts Medical School's Center For Mindfulness in Shrewsbury, MA. You may contact them by phone at 508-856-2656 or visit their website at www.umassmed.edu.

The practice of mindfulness is a systematic method of cultivating insight, clarity and understanding. It is a way of learning more of what is happening in one's life at any given moment and providing a greater sense of connection while mobilizing one's own inner resources for coping, growing and healing.

The effects of mindfulness and MBSR have been found to positively and quite often profoundly affect the ability of participants to reduce medical symptoms and psychological distress. Learning to live life more fully and enjoyably is a direct result.

148

Chapter Seven

A Life Fulfilled

One of the pivotal points in my life was when my wife, Paula, presented me with Dr. Kabat-Zinn's book *Full Catastrophe Living: Using the Wisdom of the Body and Mind to Face Stress, Pain and Illness*.

I was in the most miserable state of health that I had ever experienced, and I was frightened that I might not recover. The outcome I envisioned for myself was the worst that I could imagine. There was no improvement in sight, and I was petrified.

Without hesitation, I read the book and completed the exercises. I sacrificed time each day to devote to a meditation practice that I had no idea would work for me. At that point in my life, I was desperate and willing to try just about anything.

The results were nothing short of amazing. Three weeks into the program, my symptoms began to subside. I was concerned that this was only a short-term remission of my ulcerative colitis, but when the symptoms did not return, I was enthusiastic about the possibility of complete remission.

Over the next three months, my symptoms completely disappeared, and life became wonderfully different. I felt better than I had in many years and was gaining a sense of peace that I had never felt before.

Dr. Honer was amazed and quite pleased by the results. I discontinued all of my medications and began to enjoy life more than ever. It was the beginning of a new chapter in my life. I was learning more about myself and my life through my newfound experience with meditation, and I was overjoyed.

I found that I was the one responsible for changing my state of health and wellbeing. There was no outside force restricting my life and making me ill. I was the one in control. It was up to me and me alone to bring myself back into a healthier life.

It was in my allowing of life to unfold in a natural way that things began to move in the direction of my ultimate needs and desires. I wanted to be in good health and experience peace of mind. Meditation made this possible for me, and I am truly grateful to Jon Kabat-Zinn and his contribution to humanity.

The fast pace of society and the workplace can drain our energy and deplete our physical, mental and spiritual resources.

Most of us operate on autopilot much of the time. We cruise through the day, ignoring our inner impulses to be mindful of our existence. We hurry along, attempting to become more accomplished in our jobs and in our personal lives. We allow social media to fill the spaces between—time that we could use for quieting the mind and relaxing the body.

We find ways to occupy every second of time, reacting to the various stimuli of daily activities instead of taking advantage of free moments to recuperate and recharge our mental, emotional and physical systems.

As soon as a task is completed, we check our email, text someone, visit our social media pages or respond to any number of electronic communications. We walk to the restroom or break area with our smart-phones in hand, typing, texting or calling others with a sense of imminent importance, as if these things cannot wait another minute.

We allow ourselves to succumb to the pressures of over-booked schedules, deadlines and the demands of friends, family and coworkers for our immediate and responsive attention.

Our lives become burdened with the imagined need to respond to social requests promptly without consideration for our own need to revitalize our well-being.

We are fully capable of multi-tasking and utilizing every spare second of each minute to conquer the tasks at hand; however, our systems have been specifically designed to put forth great effort at will and then to take advantage of chances to recover and recharge.

Computers can run 24 hours a day, but they also must be re-booted occasionally to retrieve updates and to clear out unnecessary data or else their processing will slow down or become locked.

I know when I have been operating on autopilot and pushing through deadlines without sufficient breaks. I find myself stressed and depleted. My thinking becomes scattered and unfocused, my breathing becomes erratic and shallow and my digestive system presents uncomfortable consequences.

Mindfulness can bring an entirely new level of beingness into focus so that we can allow the mind and body to relax into a place of peaceful and yet effective existence.

Learning to cope with daily stress can be disconcerting to many people. Most of us did not learn how to effectively handle life's problems and difficulties at early ages. We were not taught these things growing up because our parents did not know how to deal with these issues either.

Now that mindfulness meditation and other stress-reducing techniques have come into mainstream medicine and society, it is easy to adapt and learn new ways of coping with or eliminating stress-induced illnesses.

There are many ways to counteract the onslaught of today's rapid pace of home and work-related stressors. In my first book, *The Experiential Approach*, I wrote about the power of beliefs, intentions and choices.

These three things form the foundation of our lives and are associated with everything we think, do and say. Our beliefs are the fundamental building blocks of our life's path. They guide our every move and establish the ground of the trail we walk in life.

Our intentions empower us, provide passion and drive us toward the things we desire. The choices we make direct the ultimate courses we take and determine our final destinations.

We should take inventory of our current beliefs and decide which ones need to be eliminated and what new beliefs need to be created to allow the process of life to unfold in a way in which we desire.

We need to create powerful intentions (goals) that will thrust us forward in the direction we wish to progress. They should be written down and given attention often; daily would be ideal from the outset.

Making the very best choices along the way will help us follow through with our intentions. We may need to sacrifice time away from social media, television or any number of other distractions that we may not find conducive to our progress.

Once we learn to live in each moment with a sense of mindfulness and allow ourselves to be fully present in the now, our lives will become fulfilled and more rewarding than imaginable.

Of course, this may not be as easy as making a capricious decision right now to change and live this way from here on out. Repetition is the mother of skill, and it will take practice to achieve this level of being.

That is why meditation is referred to as a practice. It takes practice, daily practice. Any skill that one wishes to attain involves some level of practice.

You may choose to begin your practice with one sitting of only 10 minutes per day, and that is perfectly reasonable. Adjustments to one's lifestyle will be required, even if they are minimal. The rewards will be great, however.

If you can commit to 10 minutes twice per day, you may gain quicker results. The more you practice and the longer you practice at each sitting, the more evident your results will be. I am referring primarily to meditation here.

Mindfulness, however, is a way of being. We can learn to be mindful in everything we do. Being mindful also produces extraordinary results.

When we can get to the point where we are in a state of mindfulness while driving, eating, talking, listening, working and playing, exercising and relaxing, life will become more exciting and more real.

Being mindful is being present, here and now. There is no place and no experience in life more important than finding ourselves in the present moment. The present is where mindfulness exists. The present is where life exists. The present is where fulfillment exists.

Visit my website at **AwakenMyPotential.com** for more information, my blog and upcoming books.

You will find my first book, **The Experiential Approach: A Fresh New Approach for Creating Immediate Personal Power**, on my website, Amazon.com and Kindle.

Resources

Dr. Andrew Weil, M.D.
drweil.com

Gaiam Life
life.gaiam.com

About.com

yoga.about.com

Self-Realization Fellowship
yogananda-srf.org

oxygen-review.com

Time
healthland.time.com

HelpGuide.org

Centers for Disease Control and Prevention
cdc.org

MedicineNet.com

Omega
eomega.com

University of Massachusetts Medical School
umassmed.edu

UCLA Health
gastro.ucla.edu

National Institute of Health and Human Services
niddk.nih.gov

Crohn's & Colitis Foundation of America
ccfa.org

Mayo Clinic
mayoclinic.org

CrohnsAndColitis.com

WebMD
webmd.com

Psychology Today
psychologytoday.com

Medical News Today
medicalnewstoday.com

Berkeley News
news.berkeley.edu

American Psychological Association
apa.org

HeartMath
heartmath.com

FreeMeditation
freemeditation.com

Huffington Post
huffingtonpost.com

I Am University of the Heart
iam-u.org

Institute of Noetic Sciences
noetic.org

Project-Meditation.org

Buddhist Society of Western Australia
dhammaloka.org.au

Vipassana Fellowship
vipassana.com

Transcendental Meditation
tm.org

Self-Guided.com

Wildmind Buddhist Meditation
wildmind.org

Zen Mountain Monastery
zmm.mro.org

Chopra Centered Lifestyle
chopra.com

Kundalini Yoga
kundaliniyoga.org

Dzogchen Center
dzogchen.org

International Dzogchen Community, Tsegyalgar East
tsegyalgar.blogspot.com

The Berlin Archives
berzinarchives.com

Mind Your Reality
mind-your-reality.com

Guided Mindfulness Meditation Practices with Jon Kabat-Zinn
mindfulnesscds.com

Mindful: Taking Time for What Matters
mindful.org

Mindfulness-Based Stress Reduction in Central Pennsylvania
meditationscience.weebly.com

Introduction to Insight Meditation
budsas.org

BrainWorks
brainworksneurotherapy.com

Mental Health Daily
mentalhealthdaily.com

HealthGrades
healthgrades.com

The American Institute of Stress
stress.org

Health Advocate
healthadvocate.com

BruceLipton.com

International Foundation for Functional Gastrointestinal Disorders
iffgd.org

aboutibs.org

healthline.com

HealthCentral.com

Copyright Dean Nelson 2014

All rights reserved

www.ingramcontent.com/pod-product-compliance
Lightning Source LLC
Chambersburg PA
CBHW060156050426
42446CB00013B/2845